REPARATIONS FOR AMERICAN SLAVERY

James Haley, *Book Editor*

Daniel Leone, *President*
Bonnie Szumski, *Publisher*
Scott Barbour, *Managing Editor*
Helen Cothran, *Senior Editor*

San Diego • Detroit • New York • San Francisco • Cleveland
New Haven, Conn. • Waterville, Maine • London • Munich

LIBRARY OF CONGRESS CATALOGING-IN-PUBLICATION DATA

Reparations for American slavery / James Haley, book editor.
   p. cm. — (At issue)
  Includes bibliographical references and index.
  ISBN 0-7377-1340-2 (lib. bdg. : alk. paper) —
  ISBN 0-7377-1341-0 (pbk. : alk. paper)
   1. African Americans—Reparations. 2. Slavery—United States—History.
I. Haley, James, 1968– . II. At issue (San Diego, Calif.)
E185.89.R45R47 2004
305.896'073—dc22   2003057736

Printed in the United States of America

Contents

Introduction

On a March 1998 tour of Africa, then-President Bill Clinton offered a "semiapology" for America's participation in the transatlantic slave trade. The president expressed regret and contrition, admitting that America had not always "done the right thing by Africa,"[1] yet he stopped short of a formal apology, asserting that to do so might antagonize race relations in the United States.[2] Slavery was permitted by law in the southern United States from the era of British colonial rule in the seventeenth century until the surrender of the Confederate secessionists following the Civil War (1861–65). Legal in Washington, D.C., slave labor was used to build the U.S. Capitol and the White House. The U.S. government, however, had never apologized to the more than 30 million African Americans living in America whose ancestors had toiled as slaves, nor had an apology been offered to the West African nations from which millions of Africans had been captured and transported on a harrowing, and often deadly, trip across the Atlantic Ocean.

What went unspoken by Clinton was the fact that a formal apology could be interpreted in a court of law as an admission of guilt by the U.S. government for sanctioning the institution of slavery. Such an admission might mean that the U.S. government could be successfully sued for *reparations* payable to the descendants of slaves. Reparations are the means by which governments and corporations make restitution—typically in cash payments—to individuals who have suffered wrongful harm as a result of negligent laws and actions. In 1988, for example, Congress passed legislation authorizing the payment of $20,000 to each Japanese American who was forcibly interned in camps on the West Coast of the United States during World War II.

Clinton's tentative steps toward a formal apology for American slavery focused national attention on the growing campaign of African American activists who are seeking reparations from both the U.S. government and the still-intact corporations that profited from the slave trade. Demands for slavery reparations have been lodged since the Civil War, but the campaign's modern incarnation took root during the civil rights movement of the 1960s. Black Muslim leader Malcolm X demanded the "forty acres and a mule" that President Andrew Johnson (1865–69) was widely believed to have promised, but never delivered, to the freed slaves. According to historian Elazar Barkan in *The Guilt of Nations*, "During the urban riots of the 1960s [black] looters claimed their loot was their forty acres and promised to be back for the mule."[3] In 1969 an organized movement for reparations coalesced following a protest staged by black activist James Foreman. Interrupting a service at the predominantly white Riverside Church in New York City, Foreman read his "Black Manifesto," which demanded that white churches and synagogues pay reparations totaling $500 million to African Americans for condoning and abetting

4

slavery. Activist groups were formed throughout the 1970s and 1980s to study and promote the issue of slavery reparations.

By 1989, the payment of reparations to Japanese Americans had encouraged Michigan Congressman John Conyers Jr. to introduce bill H.R. 40—an allusion to "forty acres and a mule"—calling for federal acknowledgement of the cruelty and injustice of slavery and a study of slavery's effects on contemporary African Americans. Conyers's bill gave the reparations movement the imprimatur of mainstream backing, but it remains in congressional committee. In the meantime, other reparations advocates have sought redress through the judicial process. In March 2002 a lawsuit was filed by Deadria C. Farmer-Paellmann in Brooklyn, New York, seeking damages payable to slave descendants from insurance and rail companies that profited from the sale and transportation of slaves. Similar lawsuits have since been filed in several other states; the outcome of these cases is still pending as of spring 2003. In addition, the Reparations Coordinating Committee (RCC), a group of prominent African American lawyers and academics, has publicly stated that it plans to file a reparations lawsuit once a legal strategy has been determined.

The campaign for slavery reparations rests on the assertion that African Americans who were never slaves are owed damages from nonblack taxpayers, the majority of whose ancestors did not own slaves. Estimates of the amount of damages owed are generally based on the percentage of America's wealth thought to have been derived from slave labor. Reparations advocates have called for damages ranging from hundreds of billions of dollars to more than $4 trillion. Depending on the terms of the settlement, African Americans might receive from $50,000 per family to $500,000 per person. As an alternative to cash payments, some activists propose that slavery reparations be used to establish a trust fund to distribute scholarships, housing and business loans, land grants, health services, and other empowerment initiatives within the African American community.

Many reparations activists address the ostensible unfairness of such a sizable transfer of wealth by arguing that the historical injustice of slavery cannot be viewed separately from the current plight of African Americans, who are still affected by the legacy of slavery and the decades of institutionalized racism that followed the Civil War. Explains John Conyers Jr., "African Americans are still victims of slavery as surely as those who lived under its confinement. . . . Just as white Americans have benefited from education, life experiences, and wealth that was handed down to them by their ancestors, so too have African Americans been harmed by the institution of slavery."[4] By this reasoning, slavery was simply replaced, in the words of Columbia University Professor Manning Marable, by a "pattern of white privilege and Black inequality that is at the core of American history and continues to this day."[5]

In the view of Conyers, Marable, and other reparations proponents, the U.S. government is directly responsible for the persistent inequality experienced by African Americans. Not only did the government condone slavery for eighty-nine years (1776–1865), it also compounded slavery's harmful legacy through its misdeeds both during and after the post–Civil War Reconstruction period. The 4 million freed slaves, who were destitute and largely illiterate, were not provided with the relief assistance and civil rights protections necessary to begin successful lives as free people following emancipation. Government proposals to provide them with abandoned and confiscated Southern lands—the "forty acres and a mule" that would have enabled economic independence from former slave masters—were scuttled by President Lincoln's successor, former vice president Andrew Johnson. With land ownership out of reach, the majority of freed people were left at the mercy of white landowners who instituted a system of sharecropping and peonage, under which freed people were forced to work off unemployment "fines" to avoid jail sentences. As black intellectual W.E.B. Du Bois maintains in "Back Toward Slavery," a chapter from his 1935 book *Black Reconstruction*, "It was the policy of the [Southern] state to keep the Negro laborer poor, to confine him as far as possible to menial occupations, . . . and to force him into peonage and unpaid toil."[6] Educational opportunities were also severely limited. Describes Du Bois, "The schools were separate but the colored schools were controlled by white officials who decided how much or rather how little should be spent upon them."[7] Southern states deprived African Americans of their basic civil rights by passing "Jim Crow" laws—named for a popular character in a minstrel show (minstrel shows were degrading performances in which whites impersonated blacks). For nearly one hundred years (1865–1964), Jim Crow laws enforced segregation in schools and places of public accommodation, denied blacks the right to vote through literacy and property ownership litmus tests, and subjected them to lynchings and other forms of mob violence that went unpunished by southern law enforcement.

According to reparations proponents, the historic disdain exhibited by the U.S. government for the civil rights of African Americans has done lasting damage to their social and economic well-being. Federal civil rights legislation, introduced in the mid-1960s, came too late to close the enormous income and personal wealth gap that arose between blacks and whites in the segregated economy of the South, where most blacks resided and where simply earning a subsistence living was difficult until the late 1960s. Beginning at this time, antipoverty programs like welfare and affirmative action—the program that gives blacks, women, and other minorities preferential treatment in some hiring, contracting, and university admissions decisions—were introduced. But reparations proponents contend that neither welfare nor affirmative action was intended for the exclusive use of African Americans, and both programs have been undermined by legislation and court decisions that limit their applicability and efficacy. The result: Contemporary African Americans inherited far fewer assets from their parents and grandparents than did their white counterparts, and they are still playing economic catch-up. Sociologists Joe R. Feagin and Eileen O'Brien explain: "African American families on average have less than one-tenth the wealth of whites. Even middle-class African Americans . . . have only fifteen cents to every middle-class white's dollar."[8]

In addition, reparations advocate Earl Ofari Hutchinson argues that racial discrimination remains a powerful hindrance to the economic success of blacks, who face rates of unemployment and poverty double those of whites. Says Hutchinson, "Slavery ended in 1865 but the legacy of slavery still remains. . . . [B]lacks are still the major economic and social victims of racial discrimination. They are far more likely to live in underserved segregated neighborhoods, be refused business and housing loans, be denied promotions in corporations and attend cash-starved, failing public schools than whites."[9] Hutchinson estimates that discrimination continues to cost blacks $10 billion annually in assets that are wrongly transferred to whites through the "the black-white wage gap, denial of capital access, inadequate public services, and reduced Social Security and other government benefits."[10] Racial discrimination and concomitant economic inequality are also cited by Randall Robinson, author of *The Debt: What America Owes to Blacks*, as the leading factors behind the disproportionately high infant mortality rate, below-average life span, and high incarceration rate of African Americans.[11] Robinson maintains that the economic gap between blacks and whites has been "resolutely nurtured" by law and public policy since the end of slavery.[12]

Based on these troubling social and economic indicators, a large transfer of wealth to African Americans is the only way that fundamental equality in American society can be achieved, according to many reparations advocates. Observes University of Maryland professor Ronald Walters, "Slavery is responsible for having robbed black people of the economic resources necessary to acquire the cultural tools and institutions of the dominant group. . . . [B]lacks are the only group expected to come all the way up the rough side of the mountain—in the most economically competitive society in the world—without the requisite resources to do so."[13]

The historical injustices committed against African Americans are undeniable, but critics of the reparations campaign do not see a connection between the wrongs of past centuries and the present economic status of black America. Conservative commentator David Horowitz strongly disagrees with Randall Robinson's assertion that since the end of slavery, public policy has done little to help blacks reach economic parity with whites. Wonders Horowitz, "After billions were spent on affirmative action programs, federal anti-discrimination laws and extensive social programs aimed at addressing racial barriers and deficits, how is it possible to say that the [economic] gap between blacks and whites has been 'resolutely nurtured' for the past 136 years?"[14] To Horowitz, Robinson conveniently ignores the irresponsible behavior that is to blame for the social pathologies besetting the black underclass. In fact, conservative critics charge that something-for-nothing programs like welfare and affirmative action—which, they argue, reparations payments would merely replicate—undermine personal responsibility and initiative and have fostered a culture of economic dependency, out-of-wedlock childbirths, and intellectual laziness that has nothing to do with the legacy of slavery. Argues conservative black commentator Shelby Steele, "I believe the greatest problem black America has had over the past 30 years has been precisely a faith in reparational uplift. . . . We fought for welfare programs that only subsidized human inertia, for cultural approaches to education that stagnated skill development in our young and for affirmative-action programs that removed the incentive to excellence in our best and brightest."[15] More handouts, this time under the banner of "slavery reparations," would only create more social and economic distress, in Steele's view.

The debate over reparations for American slavery brings to the forefront much of the racial division and resentment that has vexed America since the end of the Civil War. Proponents strongly believe that a public apology and the payment of reparations are a meaningful step toward healing the lingering damage that slavery and decades of societal discrimination have done to African Americans. However, in asking white Americans to pay for the sins of their ancestors, opponents contend, reparations advocates run the risk of driving a further wedge of racial resentment between blacks and whites, creating more problems than they solve. After all, they point out some African Americans have achieved great wealth and status and many are solidly middle class, while millions of working-class whites and recent immigrants remain on the bottom rung of the economic ladder. Contends African American journalist Deroy Murdock, "If it is wrong for a cop to eye a black man and consider him a criminal, it is equally wrong for a Treasury official to see that same man and regard him as disadvantaged and deserving of a check. . . . Ultimately, the cost in anti-black ill will that reparations would engender would outstrip any benefit from 'gaining justice' for slavery."[16]

As the movement for slavery reparations gains momentum, Americans of all races may soon have to confront this complex, controversial issue. The following articles in *At Issue: Reparations for American Slavery* offer a diverse array of opinions from leading proponents and critics engaged in the slavery reparations debate.

Notes

1. Quoted in Ronald Walters, "For Slavery?: Let's Resolve the Inequity," *World and I*, April 2000, p. 18.

2. *U.S. News & World Report*, April 6, 1998, p. 7.

3. Elazar Barkan, *The Guilt of Nations: Restitution and Negotiating Historical Injustices*. New York: W.W. Norton & Company, 2000, p. 284.

4. Quoted in Barkan, *The Guilt of Nations*, p. 292.

5. Manning Marable, "Racism and Reparations: The Time Has Come for Whites to Acknowledge the Legacy of Nearly 250 Years of Slavery and Almost 100 Years of Legalized Segregation," *Peace and Freedom*, Summer 2002, p. 20.

6. W.E. Burghardt Du Bois, *Black Reconstruction*. New York: Russell & Russell, 1935, p. 696.

7. Du Bois, *Black Reconstruction*, p. 695.

8. Joe R. Feagin and Eileen O'Brien, "The Long-Overdue Reparations for African Americans: Necessary for Societal Survival?" in *When Sorry Isn't Enough: The Controversy over Apologies and Reparations for Human Injustice*, Roy L. Brooks, ed. New York: New York University Press, 1999, p. 418.

9. Earl Ofari Hutchinson, "Ten Reasons Why Considering Reparations Is a Good Idea for Americans and Horowitz Too," *Poverty & Race*, June 30, 2001, p. 7.

10. Hutchinson, "Ten Reasons Why Considering Reparations Is a Good Idea for Americans and Horowitz Too," p. 7.

11. Randall Robinson, *The Debt: What America Owes to Blacks*. New York: Dutton, 2000, p. 62.

12. Robinson, *The Debt*, p. 204.

13. Ronald Walters, "For Slavery?: Let's Resolve the Inequity," p. 18.

14. David Horowitz, *Uncivil Wars: The Controversy over Reparations for Slavery.* San Francisco: Encounter Books, 2002, p. 109.

15. Shelby Steele, ". . . Or a Childish Illusion of Justice? Reparations Enshrine Victimhood, Dishonoring Our Ancestors," *Newsweek*, August 27, 2001, p. 23.

16. Deroy Murdock, "A Bean Counting Nightmare to Avoid," *American Enterprise*, July/August 2001, p. 23.

1

Ten Reasons Why Reparations for Slavery Are a Bad Idea

David Horowitz

David Horowitz is president of the Center for the Study of Popular Culture, a conservative think tank in Los Angeles, California. He is the author of Uncivil Wars: The Controversy over Reparations for Slavery, *the source of the following viewpoint, and* Hating Whitey and Other Progressive Causes.

Claims for slavery reparations are founded on racist ideas that are inconsistent with America's democratic principles and institutions. Singling out only white Americans as those responsible for paying reparations to the descendants of slaves is unfair since Africans were involved in the slave trade as well. Moreover, targeting all white Americans is wrong because only a tiny minority of whites ever owned slaves and many emigrants to America arrived long after slavery had ended. Trillions of dollars in reparations payments have already been paid to blacks in the form of welfare benefits and other racial preferences. In fact, African Americans owe a debt to America, since they now enjoy the highest standard of living of blacks anywhere in the world.

I. *There is no single group responsible for the crime of slavery.*
Black Africans and Arabs were responsible for enslaving the ancestors of African-Americans. There were 3,000 black slave-owners in the antebellum [era prior to the Civil War] United States. Are reparations to be paid by their descendants too? There were white slaves in colonial America. Are their descendents going to receive payments?

The impossibility of assigning blame

II. *There is no single group that benefited exclusively from slavery.*
The claim for reparations is premised on the false assumption that

David Horowitz, *Uncivil Wars: The Controversy over Reparations for Slavery.* San Francisco, CA: Encounter Books, 2002. Copyright © 2002 by David Horowitz. Reproduced by permission of the publisher, www.encounterbooks.com.

only whites have benefited from slavery. If slave labor has created wealth for Americans, then obviously it has created wealth for black Americans as well, including the descendants of slaves. The GNP [gross national product] of black America makes the African-American community the tenth most prosperous "nation" in the world. American blacks on average enjoy per capita incomes in the range of twenty to fifty times that of blacks living in any of the African nations from which they were kidnapped.

Only a tiny minority of Americans ever owned slaves. . . . Why should their descendants owe a debt?

III. *Only a minority of white Americans owned slaves, while others gave their lives to free them.*

Only a tiny minority of Americans ever owned slaves. This is true even for those who lived in the antebellum South where only one white in five was a slaveholder. Why should their descendants owe a debt? What about the descendants of the 350,000 Union soldiers who died to free the slaves? They gave their lives. What morality would ask their descendants to pay again? If paying reparations on the basis of skin color is not racism, what is?

IV. *Most living Americans have no connection (direct or indirect) to slavery.*

The two great waves of American immigration occurred after 1880 and then after 1960. What logic would require Vietnamese boat people, Russian refuseniks, Iranian refugees, Armenian victims of the Turkish persecution, Jews, Mexicans, Greeks, or Polish, Hungarian, Cambodian and Korean victims of Communism, to pay reparations to American blacks?

V. *The historical precedents used to justify the reparations claim do not apply, and the claim itself is based on race not injury.*

The historical precedents generally invoked to justify the reparations claim are payments to Jewish survivors of the Holocaust, Japanese-Americans[1] and African-American victims of racial experiments in Tuskegee, [Alabama] or racial outrages in Rosewood [Florida] and Oklahoma City [Oklahoma]. But in each case, the recipients of reparations were the direct victims of the injustice or their immediate families. This would be the only case of reparations to people who were not immediately affected and whose sole qualification to receive reparations would be racial. During the slavery era, many blacks were free men or slave-owners themselves, yet the reparations claimants make no attempt to take this fact into account. If this is not racism, what is?

VI. *The reparations argument is based on the unsubstantiated claim that all African-Americans suffer from the economic consequences of slavery and discrimination.*

No scientific attempt has been made to prove that living individuals have been adversely affected by a slave system that was ended nearly 150 years ago. But there is plenty of evidence that the hardships of slavery were hardships that individuals could and did overcome. The black mid-

---

1. Survivors of Japanese internment camps were paid reparations from the U.S. government in 1988.

dle class in America is a prosperous community that is now larger in absolute terms than the black underclass. Its existence suggests that present economic adversity is the result of failures of individual character rather than the lingering after-effects of racial discrimination or a slave system that ceased to exist well over a century ago. West Indian blacks in America are also descended from slaves but their average incomes are equivalent to the average incomes of whites (and nearly 25 percent higher than the average incomes of American-born blacks). How is it that slavery adversely affected one large group of descendants but not the other? How can government be expected to decide an issue that is so subjective?

If not for the anti-slavery beliefs . . . of white Englishmen and Americans, the slave trade would not have been brought to an end.

VII. *The reparations claim is one more attempt to turn African-Americans into victims. It sends a damaging message to the African-American community and to others.*

The renewed sense of grievance—which is what the claim for reparations will inevitably create—is not a constructive or helpful message for black leaders to send to their communities and to others. To focus the social passions of African-Americans on what some other Americans may have done to their ancestors 50 or 150 years ago is to burden them with a crippling sense of victimhood. How are the millions of non-black refugees from tyranny and genocide who are now living in America going to receive these claims, moreover, except as demands for special treatment—an extravagant new handout that is only necessary because some blacks can't seem to locate the ladder of opportunity within reach of others, many of whom are less privileged than themselves?

Debts paid and unpaid

VIII. *Reparations to African-Americans have already been paid.*

Since the passage of the Civil Rights Acts [1960, 1964, 1968] and the advent of the Great Society in 1965 [introduced by President Lyndon Johnson], trillions of dollars in transfer payments have been made to African-Americans in the form of welfare benefits and racial preferences (in contracts, job placements and educational admissions)—all under the rationale of redressing historic racial grievances. It is said that reparations are necessary to achieve a healing between African-Americans and other Americans. If trillion-dollar restitutions and a wholesale rewriting of American law (in order to accommodate racial preferences) is not enough to achieve a "healing," what is?

IX. *What about the debt blacks owe to America?*

Slavery existed for thousands of years before the Atlantic slave trade, and in all societies. But in the thousand years of slavery's existence, there never was an anti-slavery movement until white Anglo-Saxon Christians created one. If not for the anti-slavery beliefs and military power of white Englishmen and Americans, the slave trade would not have been brought to an end. If not for the sacrifices of white soldiers and a white American president [Abraham Lincoln] who gave his life [Lincoln was assassinated on April 14, 1865] to sign the Emancipation Proclamation [a declaration which freed the Confederate slaves on January 1, 1863], blacks in America would still be slaves. If not for the dedication of Americans of all ethnicities and colors to a society based on the principle that all men are created equal, blacks in America would not enjoy the highest standard of living of blacks anywhere in the world, and indeed one of the highest standards of living of any people in the world. They would not enjoy the greatest freedoms and the most thoroughly protected individual rights anywhere. Where is the acknowledgment of black America and its leaders for those gifts?

X. *The reparations claim is a separatist idea that sets African-Americans against the nation that gave them freedom.*

Blacks were here before the Mayflower. Who is more American than the descendants of African slaves? For the African-American community to isolate itself from America is to embark on a course whose implications are troubling. Yet the African-American community has had a long-running flirtation with separatists, nationalists and the political left, who want African-Americans to be no part of America's social contract. African-Americans should reject this temptation.

For all America's faults, African-Americans have an enormous stake in this country and its heritage. It is this heritage that is really under attack by the reparations movement. The reparations claim is one more assault on America, conducted by racial separatists and the political left. It is an attack not only on white Americans, but on all Americans—especially African-Americans.

America's African-American citizens are the richest and most privileged black people alive, a bounty that is a direct result of the heritage that is under assault. The American idea needs the support of its African-American citizens. But African-Americans also need the support of the American idea. For it is the American idea that led to the principles and created the institutions that have set African-Americans—and all of us—free.

2

Ten Reasons Why Reparations for Slavery Are a Good Idea

Ernest Allen Jr. and Robert Chrisman

Ernest Allen Jr., a frequent contributor to the Black Scholar, *is a professor of Afro-American studies at the University of Massachusetts in Amherst. Robert Chrisman is editor in chief of the quarterly journal* Black Scholar, *which focuses on black issues.*

David Horowitz's 2001 article on why reparations for slavery is a bad idea is an ill-informed, racist polemic against African Americans. Contrary to Horowitz's assertion that no single group can be held responsible for slavery, white Americans and their governmental institutions were the principal forces behind the transatlantic slave trade; as such, white Americans clearly benefitted most from slavery and should be charged with compensating the descendants of slaves. Moreover, welfare benefits and affirmative action programs do not count as reparations since more whites than blacks receive welfare, and affirmative action programs were put into place only after blacks sued white businesses and governments. History shows that African Americans had to fight for their freedom and owe no debt to America.

D avid Horowitz's article, "Ten Reasons Why Reparations for Slavery is a Bad Idea and Racist Too," achieved circulation [in the spring of 2001] in a handful of college newspapers throughout the United States as a paid advertisement sponsored by the Center for the Study of Popular Culture [a conservative research group]. Since then it has appeared in numerous other mainstream publications. While Horowitz's article pretends to address the issues of reparations, it is not about reparations at all. It is, rather, a well-heeled, coordinated attack on Black Americans which is calculated to elicit division and strife. Horowitz reportedly attempted to place his article in some 50 student newspapers at universities and colleges across the country, and was successful in purchasing space in such newspapers at Brown, Duke, Arizona, University of California at Berkeley, University of California at Davis, University of Chicago, and University of Wisconsin, paying an average of $700 per paper. His campaign has succeeded in fomenting outrage, dissension, and grief wherever it has appeared. Unfortunately, both its supporters and its foes too often have categorized the issue as one centering on "free speech." The sale and purchase of advertising space is not a matter of free speech, however, but involves an exchange of commodities. Professor Lewis Gordon of Brown University put it very well, saying that "what concerned me was that the ad was both hate speech and a solicitation for financial support to develop antiblack ad space. I was concerned that it would embolden white supremacists and antiblack racists." At a March 15 panel held at UC Berkeley, Horowitz also conceded that his paid advertisement did not constitute a free speech issue.

Rebutting a "racist polemic"

As one examines the text of Horowitz's article, it becomes apparent that it is not a reasoned essay addressed to the topic of reparations: it is, rather, a racist polemic against African-Americans and Africans that is neither responsible nor informed, relying heavily upon sophistry and a Hitlerian "Big Lie" technique. To our knowledge, only one of Horowitz's ten "reasons" has been challenged by a black scholar as to source, accuracy, and validity. It is our intention here to briefly rebut his slanders in order to pave the way for an honest and forthright debate on reparations. In these efforts we focus not just on slavery, but also the legacy of slavery which continues to inform institutional as well as individual behavior in the U.S. to this day. Although we recognize that white America still owes a debt to the descendants of slaves, in addressing Horowitz's distortions of history we do not act as advocates for a specific form of reparations.

The principal responsibility for . . . the institutionalization of slavery . . . rests with European and American individuals and institutions.

---

1. *There is no single group clearly responsible for the crime of slavery.*
Horowitz's first argument, relativist in structure, can only lead to two conclusions: 1) societies are not responsible for their actions and 2) since "everyone" was responsible for slavery, no one was responsible. While diverse groups on different continents certainly participated in the trade, the principal responsibility for internationalization of that trade and the institutionalization of slavery in the so-called New World rests with European and American individuals and institutions. The transatlantic slave trade began with the importation of African slaves into Hispaniola [now Haiti and the Dominican Republic] by Spain in the early 1500s. Nationals of France, England, Portugal, and the Netherlands, supported by their respective governments and powerful religious institutions, quickly entered the trade and extracted their pieces of silver as well. By conservative

estimates, 14 million enslaved Africans survived the horror of the Middle Passage [the ocean voyage to the New World] for the purpose of producing wealth for Europeans and Euro-Americans in the New World.

While there is some evidence of blacks owning slaves for profit purposes—most notably the creole caste in Louisiana—the numbers were small. As historian James Oakes noted, "By 1830 there were some 3,775 free black slaveholders across the South. . . . The evidence is overwhelming that the vast majority of black slaveholders were free men who purchased members of their families or who acted out of benevolence."

The historical precedents for the [slavery] reparations claims . . . are fully consistent with restitution accorded other historical groups.

---

2. There is no single group that benefited exclusively from slavery.

Horowitz's second point, which is also a relativist one, seeks to dismiss the argument that white Americans benefited as a group from slavery, contending that the material benefits of slavery could not accrue in an exclusive way to a single group. But such sophistry evades the basic issue: who benefited primarily from slavery? Those who were responsible for the institutionalized enslavement of people of African descent also received the primary benefits from such actions. New England slave traders, merchants, bankers, and insurance companies all profited from the slave trade, which required a wide variety of commodities ranging from sails, chandlery, foodstuffs, and guns, to cloth goods and other items for trading purposes. Both prior to and after the American Revolution [1775–83], slaveholding was a principal path for white upward mobility in the South. The white native-born as well as immigrant groups such as Germans, Scots Irish, and the like participated. In 1860, cotton was the country's largest single export.

As [historians] Eric Williams and C.L.R. James have demonstrated, the free labor provided by slavery was central to the growth of industry in western Europe and the United States; simultaneously, as [historian] Walter Rodney has argued, slavery depressed and destabilized the economies of African states. Slaveholders benefited primarily from the institution, of course, and generally in proportion to the number of slaves that they held. But the sharing of the proceeds of slave exploitation spilled across class lines within white communities as well.

As historian John Hope Franklin [has] affirmed in a rebuttal to Horowitz's claims:

> All whites and no slaves benefited from American slavery. All blacks had no rights that they could claim as their own. All whites, including the vast majority who had no slaves, were not only encouraged but authorized to exercise dominion over all slaves, thereby adding strength to the system of control.
>
> If David Horowitz had read James D. DeBow's [1860 book] *The Interest in Slavery of the Southern Nonslaveholder*, he would

not have blundered into the fantasy of claiming that no single group benefited from slavery. Planters did, of course. New York merchants did, of course. Even poor whites benefited from the legal advantage they enjoyed over all blacks as well as from the psychological advantage of having a group beneath them.

The context of the African-American argument for reparations is confined to the practice and consequences of slavery within the United States, from the colonial period on through final abolition and the aftermath, circa 1619–1865. Contrary to Horowitz's assertion, there is no record of institutionalized white enslavement in colonial America. Horowitz is confusing the indenture of white labor, which usually lasted seven years or so during the early colonial period, with enslavement. African slavery was expanded, in fact, to replace the inefficient and unenforceable white indenture system.

Most blacks suffered and continue to suffer the economic consequences of slavery and its aftermath.

Seeking to claim that African-Americans, too, have benefited from slavery, Horowitz points to the relative prosperity of African-Americans in comparison to their counterparts on the African continent. However, his argument that, "the GNP [gross national product] of black America makes the African-American community the 10th most prosperous 'nation' in the world" is based upon a false analogy. GNP is defined as "the total market value of all the goods and services produced by a nation during a specified period." Black Americans are not a nation and have no GNP. Horowitz confuses disposable income and "consumer power" with the generation of wealth.

The debt of white Americans, past and present

3. *Only a tiny minority of white Americans ever owned slaves, and others gave their lives to free them.*

Most white Union troops were drafted into the Union army in a war which the federal government initially defined as a "war to preserve the union." In large part because they feared that freed slaves would flee the South and "take their jobs" while they themselves were engaged in warfare with Confederate troops, recently drafted white conscripts in New York City and elsewhere rioted during the summer of 1863, taking a heavy toll on black civilian life and property. Too many instances can be cited where white northern troops plundered the personal property of slaves, appropriating their bedding, chickens, pigs, and foodstuffs as they swept through the South. On the other hand, it is certainly true that there also existed principled white commanders and troops who were committed abolitionists.

However, Horowitz's focus on what he mistakenly considers to be the overriding, benevolent aim of white union troops in the Civil War obscures the role that blacks themselves played in their own liberation. African-Americans were initially forbidden by the Union to fight in the Civil War, and black leaders such as Frederick Douglass and Martin Delany demanded the right to fight for their freedom. When racist doctrine finally conceded to military necessity, blacks were recruited into the Union army in 1862 at approximately half the pay of white soldiers—a situation which was partially rectified by an act of Congress in mid-1864. Some 170,000 blacks served in the Civil War, representing nearly one third of the free black population.

By 1860, four million blacks in the U.S. were enslaved; some 500,000 were nominally free. Because of slavery, racist laws, and racist policies, blacks were denied the chance to compete for the opportunities and resources of America that were available to native whites and immigrants: labor opportunities, free enterprise, and land. The promise of "forty acres and a mule" to former slaves was effectively nullified by the actions of President Andrew Johnson. And because the best land offered by the Homestead Act of 1862 and its subsequent revisions quickly fell under the sway of white homesteaders and speculators, most former slaves were unable to take advantage of its provisions.

4. *Most living Americans have no connection (direct or indirect) to slavery.*

As Joseph Anderson, member of the National Council of African-American Men, observed, "the arguments for reparations aren't made on the basis of whether every white person directly gained from slavery. The arguments are made on the basis that slavery was institutionalized and protected by law in the United States. As the government is an entity that survives generations, its debts and obligations survive the lifespan of any particular individuals. . . . Governments make restitution to victims as a group or class."

Most Americans today were not alive during World War II. Yet reparations to Japanese Americans for their internment in concentration camps during the war was paid out of current government sources contributed to by contemporary Americans. Passage of time does not negate the responsibility of government in crimes against humanity. Similarly, German corporations are not the "same" corporations that supported the Holocaust; their personnel and policies today belong to generations removed from their earlier criminal behavior. Yet, these corporations are being successfully sued by Jews for their past actions. In the same vein, the U.S. government is not the same government as it was in the pre–Civil War era, yet its debts and obligations from the past are no less relevant today.

Historical precedents and economic harm

5. *The historical precedents used to justify the reparations claim do not apply, and the claim itself is based on race not injury.*

As noted in our response to "Reason 4," the historical precedents for the reparations claims of African-Americans are fully consistent with restitution accorded other historical groups for atrocities committed against them. Second, the injury in question—that of slavery—was inflicted upon a people designated as a race. The descendants of that people—still socially constructed as a race today—continue to suffer the institutional legacies of slavery some one hundred thirty-five years after its demise. To attempt to separate the issue of so-called race from that of injury in this instance is pure sophistry. For example, the criminal (in)justice system today largely continues to operate as it did under slavery—for the protection of white citizens against black "outsiders." Although no longer inscribed in law, this very attitude is implicit to processes of law enforcement, prosecution, and incarceration, guiding the behavior of police, prosecutors, judges, juries, wardens, and parole boards. Hence, African-Americans continue to experience higher rates of incarceration than do whites charged with similar crimes, endure longer sentences for the same classes of crimes perpetrated by whites, and, compared to white inmates, receive far less consideration by parole boards when being considered for release.

Slavery was an institution sanctioned by the highest laws of the land with a degree of support from the Constitution itself. The institution of slavery established the idea and the practice that American democracy was "for whites only." There are many white Americans whose actions (or lack thereof) reveal such sentiments today—witness the response of the media and the general populace to the blatant disfranchisement of African-Americans in Florida during the last presidential election. Would such complacency exist if African-Americans were considered "real citizens"? And despite the dramatic successes of the Civil Rights movement of the 1950s and 60s, the majority of black Americans do not enjoy the same rights as white Americans in the economic sphere. (We continue this argument in the following section.)

"Welfare benefits and racial preferences" are not reparations. . . . [M]ore whites than blacks receive welfare.

---

6. *The reparations argument is based on the unfounded claim that all African-American descendants of slaves suffer from the economic consequences of slavery and discrimination.*

Most blacks suffered and continue to suffer the economic consequences of slavery and its aftermath. As of 1998, median white family income in the U.S. was $49,023; median black family income was $29,404, just 60% of white income. Further, the costs of living within the United States far exceed those of African nations. The present poverty level for an American family of four is $17,029. Twenty-three and three-fifths percent (23.6%) of all black families live below the poverty level.

When one examines net financial worth, which reflects, in part, the wealth handed down within families from generation to generation, the figures appear much starker. Recently, sociologists Melvin L. Oliver and Thomas M. Shapiro found that just a little over a decade ago, the net financial worth of white American families with zero or negative net financial worth stood at around 25%; that of Hispanic households at 54%; and that of black American households at almost 61%. The inability to accrue net financial worth is also directly related to hiring practices in which black Americans are "last hired" when the economy experiences an upturn, and "first fired" when it falls on hard times.

And as historian John Hope Franklin remarked on the legacy of slavery for black education: "laws enacted by states forbade the teaching of blacks any means of acquiring knowledge—including the alphabet—which is the legacy of disadvantage of educational privatization and discrimination experienced by African-Americans in 2001."

Horowitz's comparison of African-Americans with Jamaicans is a false analogy, ignoring the different historical contexts of the two populations. The British government ended slavery in Jamaica and its other West Indian territories in 1836, paying West Indian slave holders 20,000,000 pounds (100,000,000 U.S. dollars) to free the slaves, and leaving the black Jamaicans, who comprised 90% of that island's population, relatively free. Though still facing racist obstacles, Jamaicans come to the U.S. as voluntary immigrants, with greater opportunity to weigh, choose, and develop their options.

Seeking justice due

7. The reparations claim is one more attempt to turn African-Americans into victims. It sends a damaging message to the African-American community.

What is a victim? Black people have certainly been victimized, but acknowledgment of that fact is not a case of "playing the victim" but of seeking justice. There is no validity to Horowitz's comparison between black Americans and victims of oppressive regimes who have voluntary immigrated to these shores. Further, many members of those populations, such as Chileans and Salvadorans, direct their energies for redress toward the governments of their own oppressive nations—which is precisely what black Americans are doing. Horowitz's racism is expressed in his contemptuous characterization of reparations as "an extravagant new handout that is only necessary because some blacks can't seem to locate the ladder of opportunity within reach of others, many of whom are less privileged than themselves." What Horowitz fails to acknowledge is that racism continues as an ideology and a material force within the U.S., providing blacks with no ladder that reaches the top. The damage lies in the systematic treatment of black people in the U.S., not their claims against those who initiated this damage and their spiritual descendants who continue its perpetuation.

The discrimination in employment . . . and the widespread opposition to affirmative action . . . indicate that the vestiges of slavery are still with us.

8. Reparations to African-Americans have already been paid.

The nearest the U.S. government came to full and permanent restitution of African-Americans was the spontaneous redistribution of land brought about by General William Sherman's Field Order 15 in January, 1865, which empowered Union commanders to make land grants and give other material assistance to newly liberated blacks. But that order was rescinded by President Andrew Johnson later in the year. Efforts by

Representative Thaddeus Stevens and other radical Republicans to provide the proverbial "40 acres and a mule" which would have carved up huge plantations of the defeated Confederacy into modest land grants for blacks and poor whites never got out of the House of Representatives. The debt has not been paid.

"Welfare benefits and racial preferences" are not reparations. The welfare system was set in place in the 1930s to alleviate the poverty of the Great Depression, and more whites than blacks received welfare. So-called "racial preferences" [affirmative action] come not from benevolence but from lawsuits by blacks against white businesses, government agencies, and municipalities which practice racial discrimination.

No gratitude for historical wrongs

9. *What about the debt blacks owe to America?*

Horowitz's assertion that "in the thousand years of slavery's existence, there never was an anti-slavery movement until white Anglo-Saxon Christians created one," only demonstrates his ignorance concerning the formidable efforts of blacks to free themselves. Led by black Toussaint L'Ouverture, the Haitian revolution of 1793 overthrew the French slave system, created the first black republic in the world, and intensified the activities of black and white anti-slavery movements in the U.S. Slave insurrections and conspiracies such as those of Gabriel (1800), Denmark Vesey (1822), and Nat Turner (1831) were potent sources of black resistance; black abolitionists such as Harriet Tubman, Frederick Douglass, Richard Allen, Sojourner Truth, Martin Delany, David Walker, and Henry Highland Garnet waged an incessant struggle against slavery through agencies such as the press, notably Douglass's *North Star* and its variants, which ran from 1847 to 1863 (blacks, moreover, constituted some 75% of the subscribers to William Lloyd Garrison's *Liberator* newspaper in its first four years); the Underground Railroad, the Negro Convention Movement, local, state, and national anti-slavery societies, and the slave narrative. Black Americans were in no way the passive recipients of freedom from anyone, whether viewed from the perspective of black participation in the abolitionist movement, the flight of slaves from plantations and farms during the Civil War, or the enlistment of black troops in the Union army.

The idea of black debt to U.S. society is a rehash of the Christian missionary argument of the 17th and 18th centuries: because Africans were considered heathens, it was therefore legitimate to enslave them and drag them in chains to a Christian nation. Following their partial conversion, their moral and material lot were improved, for which black folk should be eternally grateful. Slave ideologues John Calhoun and George Fitzhugh updated this idea in the 19th century, arguing that blacks were better off under slavery than whites in the North who received wages, due to the paternalism and benevolence of the plantation system which assured perpetual employment, shelter, and board. Please excuse the analogy, but if someone chops off your fingers and then hands them back to you, should you be "grateful" for having received your mangled fingers, or enraged that they were chopped off in the first place?

10. *The reparations claim is a separatist idea that sets African-Americans against the nation that gave them freedom.*

Again, Horowitz reverses matters. Blacks are already separated from white America in fundamental matters such as income, family wealth, housing, legal treatment, education, and political representation. Andrew Hacker, for example, has argued the case persuasively in his book *Two Nations*. To ignore such divisions, and then charge those who raise valid claims against society with promoting divisiveness, offers a classic example of "blaming the victim." And we have already refuted the spurious point that African-Americans were the passive recipients of benevolent white individuals or institutions which "gave" them freedom.

Too many Americans tend to view history as "something that happened in the past," something that is "over and done," and thus has no bearing upon the present. Especially in the case of slavery, nothing could be further from the truth. As historian John Hope Franklin noted in his response to Horowitz:

> Most living Americans do have a connection with slavery. They have inherited the preferential advantage, if they are white, or the loathsome disadvantage, if they are black; and those positions are virtually as alive today as they were in the 19th century. The pattern of housing, the discrimination in employment, the resistance to equal opportunity in education, the racial profiting, the inequities in the administration of justice, the low expectation of blacks in the discharge of duties assigned to them, the widespread belief that blacks have physical prowess but little intellectual capacities and the widespread opposition to affirmative action, as if that had not been enjoyed by whites for three centuries, all indicate that the vestiges of slavery are still with us.

> And as long as there are pro-slavery protagonists among us, hiding behind such absurdities as 'we are all in this together' or 'it hurts me as much as it hurts you' or 'slavery benefited you as much as it benefited me,' we will suffer from the inability to confront the tragic legacies of slavery and deal with them in a forthright and constructive manner.

> Most important, we must never fall victim to some scheme designed to create a controversy among potential allies in order to divide them and, at the same time, exploit them for its own special purpose.

3

Americans Must Honor Their Debt to African Americans

Christopher Hitchens

Christopher Hitchens, who wrote for the Nation, *a liberal political journal, from 1982 to 2002, is a columnist at* Vanity Fair *magazine. In addition to his work as a journalist, he is a professor of liberal studies at the New School in New York City.*

Advertisements for runaway slaves carried in U.S. newspapers during the nineteenth century demonstrate that slavery was entrenched in the nation's economy. African Americans were also denied voting rights and access to property ownership until the mid-1960s. Angered by the injustice of slavery, activists are demanding that the U.S. government pay reparations—either directly or through a housing and job-training trust fund—to African Americans. The main arguments against reparations are misguided and ignore the contributions that African Americans have made to the wealth and prosperity of the United States. The country should pay reparations and be rid of the undeniable debt that is owed to African Americans.

A few years ago, I was engaged in writing an introduction to the Modern Library edition of *American Notes:* the most conservative book written by [nineteenth-century British novelist] Charles Dickens, and the only boring one. I was having a hard time with it until I came to a heart-freezing passage on slavery. Dickens in 1842 had the inspired idea of quoting directly from the "Lost and Found" classified ads of the press in the Old South, where those whose slaves had run away could advertise the fact, and those who had found stray blacks could announce likewise:

- Ran away, the negro Manuel. Much marked with irons.
- Detained at the police jail, the negro wench, Myra. Has several marks of LASHING, and has irons on her feet.
- Ran away, a negro woman and two children. A few days before she

Christopher Hitchens, "Debt of Honor," *Vanity Fair*, vol. 33, June 2001, p. 24. Copyright © 2001 by *Vanity Fair*. Reproduced by permission of the author.

went off, I burnt her with a hot iron, on the left side of her face. I tried to make the letter M.

• Ran away, my man Fountain. Has holes in his ears, a scar on the right side of his forehead, has been shot in the hind parts of his legs, and is marked on the back with the whip.

Slavery's profiteers

I now know the source from which Dickens plagiarized this chapter. It is a tract from the American Anti-Slavery Society entitled *American Slavery as It Is: Testimony of a Thousand Witnesses*. Published in New York in 1839, it is one of the most potent and lucid polemics on any subject ever printed; it's all about the moral and physical consequences of people owning other people. That same year the good ship *Amistad*, with its crew of runaway slaves, put in at New London, Connecticut. In the atmosphere of interest that was created by Steven Spielberg's movie of that drama, *The Hartford Courant*, this country's oldest newspaper, early in 2000 published an exposé of its hometown's leading industry, which is the insurance racket. It turned out that Aetna had been writing policies for slaveholders on the lives of their slaves, and doing so well into the 19th century. Score one for the *Courant*—journalism worthy of the tradition of Mark Twain, who worked on [the novel] *Huckleberry Finn* in Hartford. But then there were conniptions at the newspaper office. It also turned out that until at least 1823 the venerable sheet had carried lucrative ads not just for the sale of slaves but also for the re-capture of runaways. In July 2000, it ran a 1,500-word apology and explanation on its front page. "The stories about Connecticut's slave profiteers had a glaring omission," said the editors: "the *Courant* itself." As the story went on to say, "it was accepted practice. Slavery was so woven into the nation's economy and social fabric that such ads were probably less controversial than gun or tobacco marketing would be today."

[U.S. insurance companies wrote] policies for slaveholders on the lives of their slaves . . . well into the 19th century.

And that, as Randall Robinson would say, is more or less the point. Sitting in his office at TransAfrica [a pro-reparations research organization]—a hybrid somewhere between a think tank and a lobby—this humorous but highly determined man is launching his latest campaign. He initiated the countrywide boycott of South Africa in the 1980s, and also the moves to isolate the military dictatorships in Nigeria and Haiti. Now his book *The Debt: What America Owes to Blacks* has made the best-seller lists in Los Angeles and Washington, D.C., and in *Essence* magazine—the list to watch for African-American readership. Resolutions to reopen the debate on reparations for slavery have been passed by the city councils of Washington, Detroit, Chicago, and a growing list of other centers of population. Legal scholars such as Professor Charles Ogletree of Harvard, and legal theremust-be-a-word-for-it types like Johnnie Cochran, are getting involved.

"Show Me the Money" may be the slogan of Mr. Robert L. Brock, a veteran reparations activist who tours black audiences, tells them that each of them is owed about $500,000 for what happened to their folks, and then asks a $50 fee for his "claim form." The idea of black Americans getting a windfall from the enslavement and torture of their forebears apparently doesn't strike him as odd, though so far he and his emulators are the only ones to have made any dough from the scheme.

Robinson patiently explains that his own proposal is for a trust, set up by the federal government, from which nobody would get an individual check but by which education and housing and job training would be financed by accumulated back pay. With interest? "With interest," says Robinson. This is, after all, America.

Historical betrayals

The original proposal to compensate slaves was direct and simple. The victorious General William Tecumseh Sherman, on January 16, 1865, issued Special Field Order No. 15. It resulted in the donation to liberated slaves of "40 acres and a mule." General Rufus Saxton, who believed in the creation of a black freeholding class, supervised the distribution of land in South Carolina, while Congress ratified the order by establishing the Freedmen's Bureau to implement it and other aid to former slaves. It is still, in the collective memory of black America, a lost golden age. It didn't last long. President Andrew Johnson was one of those who thought that it was the slave*holders* who should receive compensation. (That's partly why he was later impeached.) He took the land back, and various forms of disenfranchised sharecropping and peonage became the successor system to slavery until—don't forget—the 1960s. Only two years ago [in 1999], a class-action suit against the U.S. Department of Agriculture was settled on behalf of 23,000 black farmers for the systematic denial of loans. The federal government had colluded in the writing of "restrictive" racist mortgage rules well into the 1960s.

As a result, the very means that had allowed poor immigrants from Europe to become people of property and inheritance in a generation or two—access to ownership of a plot of land or a house—were forbidden to blacks in recent living memory. And blacks are not the children of immigrants, or at least not of voluntary ones. Ever wonder how to make black Americans become incensed? Tell them to get over it because this was all a long time ago. (The great-grandchildren of the compensated Confederates, on the other hand, get all upset if you tell them that the battle flag of Robert E. Lee doesn't look so hot on the statehouse roof. Bygones be damned.)

Access to ownership of a plot of land or a house [was] . . . forbidden to blacks in recent living memory.

Jefferson Davis, first and only president of the Confederacy, was in no doubt about the main issue of the war. Even the limitation of slavery to the South, he replied to Lincoln in 1861 in justifying secession, would render "property in slaves so insecure as to be comparatively worthless . . . thereby annihilating in effect property worth thousands of millions of dollars," Lincoln himself in his second inaugural was also very conscious of the property aspect. In a brief and telling speech, he spoke of "all the wealth piled by the bondsman's two hundred and fifty years of unrequited toil," and of the "peculiar and powerful interest" represented by that one-eighth of the population held as chattel.

My friend Adolph Reed, the most caustic and witty of the black voices in print today, has ridiculed the notion of reparations in a December 2000 essay in *The Progressive:*

> On the one hand, this could promote public education about the real history of the United States, although that is a project that does not require the rhetoric of reparations. On the other hand, it fits the Clintonoid [reference to former president Bill Clinton] tenor of sappy public apologies and maudlin psychobabble about collective pain and healing. . . . Among some strains of cultural nationalists, this view unabashedly reproduces the old "damage thesis" . . . according to which slavery and its aftermath left black Americans without cultural moorings and therefore especially vulnerable to various social pathologies.

Reed's contempt for this self-pity view of history is rivaled by his scorn for the impracticalities. "Who qualifies as a recipient? Would descendants of people who had been enslaved elsewhere (for instance, Brazil or the Caribbean) be eligible? And what of those no longer legally black people with slave ancestors?"

A ten-point rebuttal

"How much?" some people ask, nervously. Jack White of *Time* magazine, who favors reviving some versions of the old Freedmen's Bureau, reckons you have to calculate unpaid wages for 10 million slaves, doubled for pain and suffering, and with interest. That would be in the trillions. The economist Larry Neal, making an inflation-adjusted guess about unpaid net wages before emancipation, arrives at a figure of about $1.4 trillion. In other words, it's not just the principle. It's the money of the thing.

Well, my health-insurance coverage (such as it is) is with Aetna. And I have recently contributed a couple of book reviews to the distinguished literary pages of *The Hartford Courant.* I came to these shores as an immigrant and have no slaveholding ancestors, but I've still benefited from the many facilities in the nation's capital that were built by unpaid labor. If I knew where to send it, or to whom, I would happily kick in a percentage of what the *Courant* paid me, in order to be quit of that debt. And I'd more than gladly change my health-insurance "carrier." However, gestures are futile. I propose the following way of making up your mind about this:

In February [2001], my old friend and enemy [conservative commentator and author] David Horowitz began placing anti-reparations ads in campus newspapers on behalf of his very conservative Center for the Study of Popular Culture. In various places—Berkeley, Brown, and Harvard among them—his ads were either rejected or apologized for by the editors

who'd printed them. In some university towns, the papers that carried the ad were stolen or destroyed. As a rebuke to this nastiness, I'll give the 10 points of his ad for free and then my own devil's-advocate response.

1. *"There is no single group responsible for the crime of slavery."*

As is well known, slaves were originally rounded up and sold by Africans and Arabs. A few thousand southern blacks became slave owners, and many poor whites were indentured. However, the Confederacy openly stated both that it was based on the principle of white supremacy and that "African slavery" was biblically warranted. (Thomas Day, who bought *The Hartford Courant* in 1855, wrote in an editorial, "We believe the Caucasian variety of the human species superior to the Negro variety; and we would breed the best stock.") Moreover, Mathieu Kerekou, president of Benin, has recently made a public apology for the part played by West Africans in enslavement, and there are dynastic fortunes in West Africa that were founded on the trade. Yes, these elements, too, should be included in the bill, if it is ever to be drawn up.

Unpaid wages for 10 million slaves, doubled for pain and suffering, and with interest . . . would be in the trillions.

---

2. *"There is no single group that benefited exclusively from slavery."*

It is true that black Americans benefit from the overall prosperity of the United States. But nobody is arguing that only white people should pay reparations. The federal government, which helped administer slavery and hunt down its fugitives, also took in much of the revenue. But it would act, if it set up a reparations trust, in a color-blind manner.

3. *"Only a minority of white Americans owned slaves, while others gave their lives to free them."*

Horowitz says that only one white person in five owned slaves in the antebellum South. Actually, J.D.B. DeBow, the superintendent of the census, took care in 1860 to emphasize that the proportion of slaveholders was closer to one-third overall, and more like one-half in rural South Carolina, Mississippi, and Louisiana. Furthermore, David Christy, author of the famous 1855 book *Cotton Is King*, made the decisive argument that the wealth of the nonslave states also derived largely from slavery. "As new grazing and grain-growing States are developed, and teem with their surplus productions, the mechanic is benefited, and the planter, relieved from food-raising, can employ his slaves more extensively on cotton. It is thus that our exports are increased; our foreign commerce advanced; the home markets of the mechanic and farmer extended, and the wealth of the nation promoted. It is thus, also, that the Free labor of the country finds remunerating markets for its products—though at the expense of serving as an efficient auxiliary in the extension of Slavery!"

4. *"Most living Americans have no connection (direct or indirect) to slavery."*

Waves of immigrants, as Horowitz points out, arrived after 1880 and 1960. But even the most impoverished Irish or Hungarians were able straightaway to join the building trades or the police departments, from which American-born were excluded. And legally enforced discrimination against the descendants of slaves persisted into the 1960s. In any case, all citizens of the country have benefited from the unrewarded heavy lifting done by kidnapped non-immigrants. Antebellum northerners, too, used to be fond of saying that they were untainted by slavery— even as they quietly reaped indirect dividends from it.

Unsubstantiated claims?

5. *"The historical precedents used to justify the reparations claim do not apply, and the claim itself is based on race not injury."*

This point has not yet been convincingly answered by the supporters of reparations, except to say that slavery was also based on race. As Adolph Reed points out, it's difficult to establish precisely who are the "descendants" of slaves. But why is that? Black Americans are of different "shades" because their maternal ancestors were raped and their paternal ones were sold down the river, and the children forcibly dispersed. Maybe we'd raise more federal and "faith-based" money if this were called reparations for violated family values.

All citizens of the country have benefited from the unrewarded heavy lifting done by kidnapped non-immigrants.

---

6. *"The reparations argument is based on the unsubstantiated claim that all African Americans suffer from the economic consequences of slavery and discrimination."*

Horowitz here points out that West Indians also suffered from slavery but, in America, achieve average incomes equal to those of whites. "How is it that slavery adversely affected one large group of descendants but not the other?" Slavery was abolished almost a generation earlier in the British Empire, and West Indians had voting rights and other liberties, with no Jim Crow [laws that enforced segregation and denied voting rights to blacks] system, well before black Americans. One might also note that, for a Republican who presumably resents the estate tax, Horowitz is strangely indifferent to the relative inability of American blacks to acquire mortgages or properties that they are able to bequeath. Derrick Jackson in *The Boston Globe* calculated that the average white baby-boomer and the average black baby-boomer can now expect to inherit, respectively, $65,000 and $8,000.

Justice Clarence Thomas, explaining recently to a high-school audience his almost complete silence in Supreme Court deliberations, said that he had been disabled by his native tongue, Gullah, in an English-speaking classroom. Gullah is a compound of West African tongues originally brought to South Carolina and Georgia by people in chains. Either this excuse was true and relevant or it was not. Horowitz might know.

7. *"The reparations claim is one more attempt to turn African Americans into victims. It sends a damaging message to the African-American community and to others."*

Undecidable.

8. *"Reparations to African Americans have already been paid."*

Welfare payments, Great Society [a 1960s welfare program, also known as the War on Poverty] programs, minority set-asides, and affirmative action are cited here. It's clear that Horowitz doesn't approve of them either. Nor does he approve of the War on Poverty in general, even though the majority of low-income Americans are white. Rural blacks in the South were excluded by law from most of the affirmative action for poor whites that was enacted during the New Deal [1930s welfare programs]. They also largely missed out, because of discrimination, on the greatest affirmative-action law ever passed, namely the 1944 G.I. Bill [provided education and other grants to veterans].

Rape, degradation, and family breakup

9. *"What about the debt blacks owe to America?"*

Smile when you say that, David. "In the thousand years of slavery's existence," he adds, "there never was an anti-slavery movement until white Anglo-Saxon Christians [Wasps] created one. . . . If not for the sacrifices of white soldiers and a white American president who gave his life to sign the Emancipation Proclamation [which freed the Confederate slaves on January 1, 1863], blacks in America would *still* be slaves."

It would be just as true to say that Christians didn't turn against slavery for almost two millennia: the first anti-slavery petition in America or anywhere else was drawn up by the Quakers of Germantown, Pennsylvania, in 1688. Then there were Thomas Paine (white and Anglo-Saxon but not Christian) and Frederick Douglass (black, probably fathered by his mother's owner, highly critical of Christian hypocrisy). The Wasp abolitionists in general believed that slavery was a curse and a sin that it would take (note this) many generations to erase. This was because of the rape and degradation and deliberate family breakup that it involved. Mr. [Abraham] Lincoln [assassinated on April 14, 1865] (see above) outlived the Emancipation Proclamation by 15 months and signed it only as a limited war measure.

Many blacks, it goes without saying, are tenaciously proud Americans and fought for the Union and the country even when (as from 1863 to 1949) they were allowed to do so only in segregated units.

> *[Paying reparations] could be an excellent way of revisiting the past and seeing . . . what can be salvaged or repaired.*

10. *"The reparations claim is a separatist idea that sets African-Americans against the nation that gave them freedom."*

Maybe this would have been better as a nine-point statement. But see above. What is clear is that the argument has now begun. If it is well conducted, it could be an excellent way of revisiting the past and seeing what may be learned from it, as well as what can be salvaged or repaired. This is a generous society as well as a litigious one. The proportions of these qualities will count; the dispute could easily become boring and rancorous, or enlightening and clarifying. Most people, even in liberal Hartford, had until recently no idea how close to the surface the bones lay. Here is what Thomas Jefferson [U.S. president 1801–09] wrote in his *Notes on Virginia*, coolly observing the slaves he owned but never emancipated, and from whom he produced off-the-record and deniable presidential children:

> They secrete less by the kidneys, and more by the glands of the skin, which gives them a very strong and disagreeable odor. . . . They are at least as brave, and more adventuresome. . . . Their griefs are transient.

In Mr. Jefferson's beloved Virginia, until 1967, marriage between blacks and whites was prohibited by law, and sterilization of "inferior" types was practiced by medical men under state warrant until 1979. There is hardly a black American whose grandmother couldn't tell him or her a personal story that would harrow the soul. Some of these griefs are beyond repair, but it would be rash and indeed impolite ever to refer to them as "transient."

4

Americans Have Paid Their Debt to African Americans

Karl Zinsmeister

Karl Zinsmeister is the J.B. Fuqua Fellow at the American Enterprise Institute (AEI), a conservative think tank based in Washington, D.C. He is also the editor in chief of AEI's monthly magazine, the American Enterprise.

The campaign seeking the payment of slavery reparations to the descendants of African American slaves is gaining momentum through the involvement of prominent lawyers, activists, and the public. While reparations should have been paid immediately following the Civil War, identifying who should pay and receive reparations is now impossible. After all, the majority of Americans living today have ancestors who were neither slaves nor slave masters or have members of both groups in their family trees. Most important, America has already paid for the sin of slavery; more than 620,000 Americans died in the struggle to end slavery during the Civil War, and the country has since provided income support, education, and special programs to African Americans.

The activist campaign demanding payment of "slavery reparations" to today's black Americans probably strikes some readers as too far-fetched to take seriously. Better stop and look afresh. I myself realized that the concept had moved beyond faculty lounges, radical salons, and afrocentric pamphlets and into the realm of serious political struggle when I looked over the roster of a legal group convened to plot practical strategy for winning such compensation. It included not only Dream Teamer [the legal team that defended accused murderer O.J. Simpson in 1994] Johnny Cochran, Harvard Law School professor Charles Ogletree, and other ideologically predictable backers, but also one Richard J. Scruggs.

From pipe dream to popular demand

Scruggs is a white Mississippi trial lawyer with a single interest: causes which have a good chance of winning him lots of money. He is in the process of

collecting billions of dollars (literally) for his part in the 1998 tobacco settlement. He is next trying to shake down HMOs [health maintenance organ-
izations] and other unpopular businesses with the threat of legal action. He
has his finger in dozens of other polemicized class-action suits. Scruggs also
happens to be the brother-in-law of Republican Senator Trent Lott. When legal vultures like Scruggs, Dennis Sweet (hyper rich from Fen-phen diet pill
[diet supplements thought to cause health problems] suits), and class-action
specialists Willie Gary and Alexander Pires begin to circle—they're all cur-
rently members of a "Reparations Assessment Group" which has both government and major corporations in its sights—some juicy carcass is usually
about to be picked clean.

---

*Reparations [are] . . . a good idea whose time has
come and long since gone.*

There are other hints that the push for payments to slave descendants
is gaining momentum. Over the last year [2000/2001], a dozen big-city
councils have passed resolutions calling on the federal government to in-
vestigate reparations payments. Representative John Conyers has a bill
[H.R. 40—the Reparations Study Bill] in Congress that would require that.
Representative Tony Hall, a white born-again Christian, is pushing a different proposal that would take up reparations; Republican congressman
J.C. Watts has expressed guarded support. Quasi-conservative *Washington
Post* columnist Charles Krauthammer wrote a column in April [2001]
proposing to give African-American families a lump sum of $50,000 each.

Among blacks on the street, meanwhile, interest in reparations is shift-
ing from pipe dream to popular demand. When I was in Dallas [in 2000] I
heard hortatory ads by pro-reparations groups on black radio stations.
Longstanding activist calls for black taxpayers to deduct "slavery credits"
from their tax payments are being heeded by more African Americans. The
IRS [Internal Revenue Service] field office responsible for the region
stretching just from northern Virginia to Delaware received 500 tax returns
claiming such a credit (illegitimately) in 2000. "We're not talking about
welfare. We're talking about back pay," is how the executive editor of
Ebony magazine now describes reparations. Overall, polls show that most
black Americans support having the government make slavery-restitution
payments—in some surveys by considerably more than two-to-one.

This subject is not going to just quietly go away, as many Americans
probably wish it would. The question must be faced. Are there merits to
the case for slavery reparations?

Squandered opportunities

I myself would characterize reparations as a good idea whose time has
come and long since gone. In the years leading up to the Civil War [1861–
65] there were various proposals for ending slavery through government
payments. [President Abraham] Lincoln called for federal compensation
to states according to the number of slaves they emancipated. A portion
of these payments could have been used to help the freed blacks establish

themselves in a new life. Unfortunately, nothing came of this.

After financial dickering gave way to war, Union General William Sherman issued his famous field order [Special Field Order, No. 15, January 16, 1865] decreeing that all freed slaves should be issued a mule and forty acres of land appropriated from plantation owners. But this was later countermanded. Much to the frustration of Republicans, new President Andrew Johnson vetoed such payments.

The result—a miserable one for blacks and for our nation—was that slaves, though liberated, were not provided any resources to help them transform themselves into self-supporting Americans. The "new Negro," [former slave and black intellectual] Frederick Douglass wrote, "had neither money, property, nor friends. He was free from the old plantation, but he had nothing but the dusty road under his feet. . . . He was turned loose naked, hungry, and destitute to the open sky."

If cash had been spent as it should have been in the 1850s or '60s on reparations to slaves and indemnities to slaveowners, a terrible war might have been avoided. If money had been spent as it should have been during early Reconstruction [the period of North/South reunification following the Civil War] to help the victims of slavery get themselves on their feet, a subsequent century of degrading poverty and segregation among blacks could have been mitigated.

But those opportunities were squandered, and there is no way to get them back. As black economist Walter Williams summarizes, "Slavery was a gross violation of human rights. Justice would demand that slave owners make compensatory reparation payments to slaves. Yet since both slaves and slave owners are no longer with us, compensation is beyond our reach."

Slave reparations . . . would . . . be a case of individuals who were never slaveholders giving money to people who were never slaves.

Ah, but even with all the parties involved long dead, couldn't we make some sort of cleansing payment that would set things right? The answer is no. The two favorite models for slave reparations—payments to Holocaust victims and interned Japanese-Americans—are utterly different situations, because in those cases the injured parties and the injurers are still alive, and able to make direct restitution, one to another.

Meanwhile the identities of "slave" and "slaveholder" have blurred and melted away over the generations to the point where it is now impossible to say who would pay and who would receive in any accounting for slavery. There are plenty of Americans who have members of both groups in their family trees. The vast majority of us have neither—we weren't slaves; we weren't slave masters. Indeed, the majority of today's Americans descend from people who were not even in America when slavery was practiced. And of the people who were here, a much larger number fought against slavery than practiced it.

It gets even messier than that. There were, for instance, approximately 12,000 black freemen living in the Confederacy who themselves owned slaves. Moreover, most of the individuals who came to America as slaves were dispatched into that state by other blacks in Africa. Who owes whom what in these cases?

Remembering the costs of the Civil War

The villains and the heroes of slavery have evaporated into the misty vapors of our past, and are now impossible to delineate clearly or bring to justice. Trying to pay slave reparations in our current decade would, as one observer puts it, mostly be a case of individuals who were never slaveholders giving money to people who were never slaves. A clear absurdity.

Political scientist Adolph Reed wrote in *The Progressive* in December 2000 that the only certain result of a reparations program would be to "produce a lively trade for genealogists, DNA testers, and other such quacks." Even Holocaust reparations—which are much simpler transfers directly to still-living victims—have turned extraordinarily unseemly and debasing. As Gabriel Schoenfeld noted recently in *Commentary*, "In the free-for-all to obtain Holocaust victims as clients . . . competing lawyers from the United States have barnstormed across Europe soliciting clients, publicly castigating each other, and privately maneuvering to oust their adversaries." If you think a subject as somber as slavery wouldn't be exploited (and ultimately decay into grasping, self-serving tawdriness) the second financial opportunism became possible, think again.

American blacks would take little solace from simply being told it's too late for restitution, that practical impossibilities leave reparations for slavery out of reach. But that's not the whole story. The whole truth, which ought to offer black America real peace, is that the United States already made a mighty payment for the sin of slavery. It was called the Civil War.

I first decided to put together [an *American Enterprise* magazine] issue on this subject almost exactly two years ago, when my hometown newspaper ran a Memorial Day ad honoring local men who had been killed in America's wars. The ad listed the names of 85 individuals who had died fighting the Civil War. I later did some research and discovered that the complete total for the three small towns that comprise our local school district was 105 killed.

In all, more than 620,000 Americans died in the struggle to eliminate slavery.

The thing you need to know to put that figure in perspective is that our rural village contains less than 3,000 people (and was not much different then). The surrounding towns add a couple thousand more. For our little community to have offered up 105 young men to be swallowed by the grave—most all of them between 18 and 29, the records show—was a great sacrifice.

Cazenovia's example was not a bit unusual. In all, more than 620,000 Americans died in the struggle to eliminate slavery. That is more than the number killed in all of our other wars combined. It amounted to a staggering 1.8 percent of our total population in 1865. That would be the equivalent of killing more than 5 million young Americans today.

The crux that defined and drove this ferocious fratricide was a determination to purge ourselves of slavery. It would be hard to overstate the pain and pathos involved in bringing that decision to its conclusion. President Lincoln's own family is an example: No fewer than seven of his brothers-in-law fought for the Confederacy; two were killed in battle. Yet Lincoln never wavered in doing what was right.

A bill paid in blood and money

Though they are often now ignored, our nation is peppered with many powerful Civil War memorials. . . . [A] monument [is] located down the road from my own home in New York state. Erected by a village of about 5,000 people, it hints at the magnitude of feeling which went into America's struggle to end enforced servitude. Our nation surely did run up a "debt" (as reparations advocates like Randall Robinson . . . like to put it) for allowing black bondage. But that bill was finally paid off, in blood.

And not only in blood. After tardily recognizing their error, Americans have tried to compensate for the historic harm visited upon African Americans. The massive infusions of money into income support, education, and special programs to benefit blacks that activists like Robinson are now calling for have already been offered up. Economist Walter Williams notes that over the last generation the American people have particularly targeted the black underclass with more than $6.1 trillion in antipoverty spending. Private and governmental agencies have tried to improve black socioeconomic status with measures ranging from affirmative action to massive philanthropic efforts. . . . American blacks have made remarkable progress.

But to the activists, this is not nearly enough. Perhaps there can never be enough done to placate them, because many are driven by an implacable sense of grievance more than a practical desire to see blacks flourish. In his book *The Debt*, [pro-reparations activist] Randall Robinson insists that blacks do not like America, and cannot be part of it. It's clear that is his own posture, and he actively urges other African Americans to share it. "You are owed," he tells his audience. "*They* did this to you" (with the italic emphasis in his text).

This is a poisonous political path. It will be psychologically unhealthy for many blacks, and it is very likely to inspire a nasty backlash among other Americans. In his thorough article on Holocaust reparations (which, again, are far more solidly founded, because the actual victims are still with us) Gabriel Schoenfeld points out that renewed pressure on Europeans over Nazi-era atrocities has unleased on that continent "a tide of anti-Semitic feeling unseen since the pre–World War II era." Aggressive reparations demands have created resentment both among intellectuals and on the streets, in the political arena as well as in social life.

Rehashing historical offenses is rarely constructive—especially since there are so many, extending in all directions and involving all races and groups. Despite the common references to slavery as America's "peculiar institution," the reality is that until the early nineteenth century there was hardly a country on earth without some kind of institutionalized slavery. One of my great-great-great-grandfathers, Mark Staggers, arrived here from England as a "bound boy"—in an indentured servitude which lasted for the rest of his childhood and much of his young adult years. My German ancestors were poor tenant farmers—the European equivalent of sharecroppers—who were repeatedly abused by Napoleon during the very years when U.S. slavery was at its peak.

Human bondage was not an American invention, it was a condition suffered by many people in many places across time. The northern U.S. states that outlawed slavery were among the first governments on the globe to do so. Rather than being some unique American stain, slavery was actually a commonplace sin, and almost six generations have now passed since it was outlawed throughout our land.

No perfect accounting

And balancing the ugliness of historical slavery in our country is the contemporary reality of enormous freedom and opportunity. Reparations activists will never say it so I will: Despite some harsh imperfections, America has, on the whole, been good to blacks, just as it has been good to other struggling groups who washed up on these shores. As economist Williams writes: "Most black Americans are middle class. And almost every black American's income is higher as a result of being born in the United States than in any country in Africa."

In the process of taming the wilderness, America's Anglo pioneers suffered heavily from human cruelty, natural disaster, disease, and deprivation. Even the most successful families sacrificed over and over. Of the 56 men who signed the Declaration of Independence to launch America, nine died of wounds or hardship during the Revolutionary War [1775–83], five were captured or imprisoned, many had wives and children who were killed or imprisoned, 12 had their houses burned to the ground, 17 lost everything they owned, a number died bankrupt and in rags.

Those who followed bore other burdens. The Irish were felled in great numbers building our first canals and railways. Southern Europeans, Asians, Hispanics, and many other immigrants endured long indignities and drudging work helping to civilize a new land. The American society that sprang from the hardships endured by our ancestors now belongs to each of us—very much including blacks, who were some of our earliest arrivals.

There is no perfect accounting in the cosmos, and none of us sitting here in twenty-first-century America really did much to "deserve" the prosperity, pleasure, and long life that our country presently allows (to the great envy of the rest of humanity). We—including those of us who are black—are just lucky to be able to profit from those earlier sacrifices.

The American blessing is available today to every citizen, regardless of how rocky our family's entry into the country. There is no "us" or "them" to give manna, or take it, only a heavily interwoven "we" who share a common interest in the success of our one system. The ultimate compensation America offers current residents is a seat in the free-est and richest society yet created by man. It's the final payment, a gift to one and all.

5

Reparations Should Be Paid to Help Reduce African American Poverty

Randall Robinson

Randall Robinson is the author of The Debt: What America Owes to Blacks, *a widely read book on the issue of slavery reparations, and the source of the following viewpoint. From 1979 to 2001 he served as founder and president of TransAfrica, a research group that analyzes U.S. policy in Africa, the Caribbean, and Latin America.*

African Americans must be compensated by the U.S. government for the centuries of unpaid labor they gave the nation and for the human rights crimes that were perpetrated upon them during and after slavery. Ex-slaves in the aftermath of the Civil War were left destitute and at the mercy of white Southerners, who, for decades, denied blacks the right to own land, vote, and receive an adequate education. As a result, educational failure and poverty has become a vicious cycle within the African American community, as successive generations of African Americans struggle to succeed. Black males are now far more likely than whites to be unemployed or incarcerated—a direct legacy of the 246-year practice of slavery. America should admit its role in the tragic condition of today's African American community.

In the early 1970s Boris Bittker, a Yale Law School professor, wrote a book, *The Case for Black Reparations*, which made the argument that slavery, Jim Crow [laws and codes that enforced segregation and denied voting rights to blacks], and a general climate of race-based discrimination in America had combined to do grievous social and economic injury to African Americans. He further argued that sustained government-sponsored violations had rendered distinctions between *de jure* and *de facto* segregation meaningless for all practical purposes. Damages, in his view, were indicated in the form of an allocation of resources to some program that could be crafted for black reparations. The book evoked little in the way of scholarly response or follow-up.

America's unpaid debt

The slim volume was sent to me by an old friend who once worked for me at TransAfrica, Ibrahim Gassama, now a law professor at the University of Oregon [at Eugene]. I had called Ibrahim in Eugene to talk over the legal landscape for crafting arguments for a claim upon the federal and state governments for restitution or reparations to the derivative victims of slavery and the racial abuse that followed in its wake.

"It's the strangest thing," Ibrahim had said to me. "We law professors talk about every imaginable subject, but when the issue of reparations is raised among white professors, many of whom are otherwise liberal, it is met with silence. Clearly, there is a case to be made for this as an unpaid debt. Our claim may not be enforceable in the courts because the federal government has to agree to allow itself to be sued. In fact, this will probably have to come out of the Congress as other American reparations have. Nonetheless, there is clearly a strong case to be made. But, I tell you, the mere raising of the subject produces a deathly silence, not unlike the silence that greeted the book I'm sending you."

[Law professor and black activist] Derrick Bell, who was teaching at Harvard Law School while I was a student there in the late 1960s, concluded his review of Bittker's book in a way that may explain the reaction Ibrahim got from his colleagues:

> Short of a revolution, the likelihood that blacks today will obtain direct payments in compensation for their subjugation as slaves before the Emancipation Proclamation [President Abraham Lincoln's declaration that freed the slaves on January 1, 1863], and their exploitation as quasi-citizens since, is no better than it was in 1866, when [Pennsylvania congressman] Thaddeus Stevens recognized that his bright hope of "forty acres and a mule" for every freedman had vanished "like the baseless fabric of a vision."

If Bell is right that African Americans will not be compensated for the massive wrongs and social injuries inflicted upon them by their government, during and after slavery, then there is *no* chance that America can solve its racial problems—if solving these problems means, as I believe it must, closing the yawning economic gap between blacks and whites in this country. The gap was opened by the 246-year practice of slavery. It has been resolutely nurtured since in law and public behavior. It has now ossified. It is structural. Its framing beams are disguised only by the counterfeit manners of a hypocritical governing class.

For twelve years [before and during World War II] Nazi Germany inflicted horrors upon European Jews. And Germany paid. It paid Jews individually. It paid the state of Israel. For two and a half centuries, Europe and America inflicted unimaginable horrors upon Africa and its people. Europe not only paid nothing to Africa in compensation, but followed the slave trade with the remapping of Africa for further European economic exploitation. (European governments have yet even to accede to Africa's request for the return of Africa's art treasures looted along with its natural resources during the century-long colonial era.)

While President Abraham Lincoln supported a plan during the Civil

War to compensate slave owners for their loss of "property," his successor, Andrew Johnson, vetoed legislation that would have provided compensation to ex-slaves.

Under the Southern Homestead Act [of 1866], ex-slaves were given six months to purchase land at reasonably low rates without competition from white southerners and northern investors. But, owing to their destitution, few ex-slaves were able to take advantage of the homesteading program. The largest number that did were concentrated in Florida, numbering little more than three thousand. The soil was generally poor and unsuitable for farming purposes. In any case, the ex-slaves had no money on which to subsist for months while waiting for crops, or the scantest wherewithal to purchase the most elementary farming implements. The program failed. In sum, the United States government provided no compensation to the victims of slavery.

Fighting for what is due

Perhaps I should say a bit here about why the question of reparations is critical to finding a solution to our race problems.

This question—and how blacks gather to pose it—is a good measure of our psychological readiness as a community to pull ourselves abreast here at home and around the world. I say this because no outside community can be more interested in solving our problems than we. Derrick Bell suggested in his review of Bittker's book that the white power structure would never support reparations because to do so would operate against its interests. I believe Bell is right in that view. The initiative must come from blacks, broadly, widely, implacably.

But what exactly will black enthusiasm, or lack thereof, measure? There is no linear solution to any of our problems, for our problems are not merely technical in nature. By now, after 380 years of unrelenting psychological abuse, the biggest part of our problem is inside us: in how we have come to see ourselves, in our damaged capacity to validate a course for ourselves without outside approval.

> *The yawning economic gap between blacks and whites in [the United States] . . . was opened by the 246-year practice of slavery.*

The issue here is not whether or not we can, or will, win reparations. The issue rather is whether we will fight for reparations, because we have decided for ourselves that they are our due. In 1915, into the sharp teeth of southern Jim Crow hostility, Cornelius J. Jones filed a lawsuit against the United States Department of the Treasury in an attempt to recover sixty-eight million dollars for former slaves. He argued that, through a federal tax placed on raw cotton, the federal government had benefited financially from the sale of cotton that slave labor had produced, and for which the black men, women, and children who had produced the cotton had not been paid. Jones's was a straightforward proposition. The monetary value of slaves' labor, which he estimated to be sixty-eight million dollars, had been appropriated by the United States government. A debt existed. It had to be paid to the, by then, ex-slaves or their heirs.

Where was the money?

A federal appeals court held that the United States could not be sued without its consent and dismissed the so-called Cotton Tax case. But the court never addressed Cornelius J. Jones's question about the federal government's appropriation of property—the labor of blacks who had worked the cotton fields—that had never been compensated.

Black people worked long, hard, killing days, years, centuries—and they were never paid.

Let me try to drive the point home here: through keloids of suffering, through coarse veils of damaged self-belief, lost direction, misplaced compass, shit-faced resignation, racial transmutation, black people worked long, hard, killing days, years, centuries—and they were never *paid*. The value of their labor went into others' pockets—plantation owners, northern entrepreneurs, state treasuries, the United States government.

Where was the money?

Where *is* the money?

There is a debt here.

I know of no statute of limitations either legally or morally that would extinguish it. Financial quantities are nearly as indestructible as matter. Take away here, add there, interest compounding annually, over the years, over the whole of the twentieth century.

Where is the money?

Jews have asked this question of countries and banks and corporations and collectors and any who had been discovered at the end of the slimy line holding in secret places the gold, the art, the money that was the rightful property of European Jews before the Nazi terror. Jews have demanded what was their due and received a fair measure of it.[1]

The legacy of unimaginable cruelties

Clearly, how blacks respond to the challenge surrounding the simple demand for restitution will say a lot more about us *and do a lot more for us* than the demand itself would suggest. We would show ourselves to be responding as any normal people would to victimization were we to assert collectively in our demands for restitution that, for 246 years and with the complicity of the United States government, hundreds of millions of black people endured unimaginable cruelties—kidnapping, sale as livestock, deaths in the millions during terror-filled sea voyages, backbreaking toil, beatings, rapes, castrations, maimings, murders. We would begin a healing of our psyches were the most public case made that whole peoples lost religions, languages, customs, histories, cultures, children, moth-

---

1. In 1977, Swiss banks paid restitution to Holocaust victims whose assets were hidden by Nazis in Swiss bank accounts.

ers, fathers. It would make us more forgiving of ourselves, more self-approving, more self-understanding to see, *really see*, that on three continents and a string of islands, survivors had little choice but to piece together whole new cultures from the rubble shards of what theirs had once been. And they were never made whole. And never compensated. Not one red cent.

Left behind to gasp for self-regard in the vicious psychological wake of slavery are history's orphans played by the brave black shells of their ancient forebears, people so badly damaged that they cannot *see* the damage, or how their government may have been partly, if not largely, responsible for the disabling injury that by now has come to seem normal and unattributable.

Until America's white ruling class accepts the fact that the book never closes on massive unredressed social wrongs, America can have no future as one people. Questions must be raised, to American private, as well as public institutions. Which American families and institutions, for instance, were endowed in perpetuity by the commerce of slavery? And how do we square things with slavery's modern victims from whom all natural endowments were stolen? What is a fair measure of restitution for this, the most important of all American human rights abuses?

If one leaves aside the question of punitive damages to do a rough reckoning of what might be fair in basic compensation, we might look first at the status of today's black male.

For purposes of illustration, let us picture one representative individual whose dead-end crisis in contemporary America symbolizes the plight of millions. At various times in his life he will likely be in jail or unemployed or badly educated or sick from a curable ailment or dead from violence.

What happened to him? From what did he emerge?

His great-great-grandfather was born a slave and died a slave. Great-great-grandfather's labors enriched not only his white southern owner but also shipbuilders, sailors, ropemakers, caulkers, and countless other northern businesses that serviced and benefited from the cotton trade built upon slavery. Great-great-grandfather had only briefly known his mother and father before being sold off from them to a plantation miles away. He had no idea where in Africa his people had originally come from, what language they had spoken or customs they had practiced. Although certain Africanisms—falsetto singing, the ring shout, and words like *yam*—had survived, he did not know that their origins were African.

He was of course compulsorily illiterate. His days were trials of backbreaking work and physical abuse with no promise of relief. He had no past and no future. He scratched along only because some biological instinct impelled him to survive.

No money, no work, no land

His son, today's black male's great-grandfather, was also born into slavery and, like his father, wrenched so early from his parents that he could scarcely remember them. At the end of the Civil War, he was nineteen years old. While he was pleased to no longer be a slave, he was uncertain that the new status would yield anything in real terms that was very much different from the life (if you could call it that) that he had been living. He too was illiterate and completely without skills.

He was one of four million former slaves wandering rootlessly around in the defeated South. He trusted no whites, whether from the North or South. He had heard during the war that even President Lincoln had been urging blacks upon emancipation to leave the United States en masse for colonies that would be set up in Haiti and Liberia [a country in West Africa settled by former slaves]. In fact, Lincoln had invited a group of free blacks to the White House in August 1862 and told them: "Your race suffers greatly, many of them, by living among us, while ours suffer from your presence. In a word we suffer on each side. If this is admitted, it affords a reason why we should be separated."

Until America's white ruling class accepts [slavery's] . . . massive unredressed social wrongs, America can have no future as one people.

Today's black male's great-grandfather knew nothing of Haiti or Liberia, although he had a good idea why Lincoln wanted to ship blacks to such places. By 1866 his life had remained a trial of instability, and rootlessness. He had no money and little more than pickup work. He and other blacks in the South were faced as well with new laws that were not unlike the antebellum Slave Codes. The new measures were called Black Codes and, as John Hope Franklin noted in *From Slavery to Freedom*, they all but guaranteed that

> the control of blacks by white employers was about as great as that which slaveholders had exercised. Blacks who quit their job could be arrested and imprisoned for breach of contract. They were not allowed to testify in court except in cases involving members of their own race. Numerous fines were imposed for seditious speeches, insulting gestures or acts, absence from work, violating curfew, and the possession of firearms. There was, of course, no enfranchisement of blacks and no indication that in the future they could look forward to full citizenship and participation in a democracy.

Although some blacks received land in the South under the Southern Homestead Act of 1866, the impression that every ex-slave would receive "forty acres and a mule" as a gift of the government never became a reality. Great-grandfather, like the vast majority of the four million former slaves, received nothing and died penniless in 1902—but not before producing a son who was born in 1890 and later became the first of his line to learn to read.

Two decades into the new century, having inherited nothing in the way of bootstraps with which to hoist himself, and faced with unremitting racial discrimination, Grandfather became a sharecropper on land leased from whites whose grandparents had owned at least one of his forebears. The year was 1925 and neither Grandfather nor his wife was allowed to vote. His son would join him in the cotton fields under the broiling sun of the early 1930s. They worked twelve hours or more a day and barely eked out a living. Grandfather had managed to finish the fifth grade before leaving school to work full time. Inasmuch as he talked like the people he knew, and like his parents and their parents before them, his syntax and pronunciation bore the mark of the unlettered. Grandfather wanted badly that his son's life not mirror his, but was failing depressingly in producing for the boy any better opportunity than that with which he himself had been presented. Not only had he no money, but he survived against the punishing strictures of southern segregation that allowed for blacks the barest leavings in education, wages, and political freedom. He was trapped and afraid to raise his voice against a system that in many respects resembled slavery, now a mere seventy years gone.

Grandfather drank and expressed his rage in beatings administered to his wife and his son. In the early 1940s Grandfather disappeared into a deep depression and never seemed the same again.

White privilege, black poverty

Grandfather's son, the father of today's black male, periodically attended segregated schools, first in a rural area near the family's leased cotton patch and later in a medium-sized segregated southern city. He learned to read passably but never finished high school. He was not stigmatized for this particular failure because the failure was not exceptional in the only world that he had ever known.

"[Following emancipation] the control of blacks by white employers was about as great as that which slaveholders had exercised."

Ingrained low expectation, when consciously faced, invites impenetrable gloom. Thus, Father did not dwell on the meagerness of his life chances. Any penchant he may have had for introspection, like his father before him, he drowned in corn spirits on Friday nights. He was a middle-aged laborer and had never been on first-name terms with anyone who was not a laborer like himself. He worked for whites and, as far as he could tell, everyone in his family before him had. Whites had, to him, the best of everything—houses, cars, schools, movie theaters, neighborhoods. Black neighborhoods he could tell from simply looking at them, even before he saw the people. And it was not just that the neighborhoods were poor. No, he had subconsciously likened something inside himself, a jagged rent in his ageless black soul, to the sagging wooden tenement porches laden with old household objects—ladders, empty flowerpots, wagons—that rested on them, often wrong side up, for months at a time. The neighborhoods, lacking sidewalks, streetlights, and sewage systems, had, like Father and other blacks, preserved themselves by not caring. Hunkered down. Gone inside themselves, turning blank, sullen faces to the outside world.

The world hadn't bothered to notice.

Father died of heart disease at the age of forty-five just before the Voting Rights Act was passed in 1965. Like his ancestors who had lived and died in slavery in centuries before, he was never allowed to cast a vote in his life. Little else distinguished his life from theirs, save a subsistence wage, the freedom to walk around in certain public areas, and the ability to read a newspaper, albeit slowly.

Parallel lines never touch, no matter how far in time and space they extend.

The black male is far more likely than his white counterpart to be in prison, to be murdered, to have no job, to fail in school, to become seriously ill.

They had been declared free—four million of them. Some had simply walked off plantations during the war in search of Union forces. Others had become brazenly outspoken to their white masters toward the war's conclusion. Some had remained loyal to their masters to the end. Abandoned, penniless and unskilled, to the mercies of a humiliated and hostile South, millions of men, women, and children trudged into the false freedom of the Jim Crow South with virtually nothing in the way of recompense, preparation, or even national apology.

It is from this condition that today's black male emerged.

His social crisis is so alarming that the United States Commission on Civil Rights by the spring of 1999 had made it the subject of an unusual two-day conference. "This is a very real and serious and difficult issue," said Mary Frances Berry, chair of the commission. "This crisis has broad implications for the future of the race."

The black male is far more likely than his white counterpart to be in prison, to be murdered, to have no job, to fail in school, to become seriously ill. His life will be shorter by seven years, his chances of finishing high school smaller—74 percent as opposed to 86 percent for his white counterpart. Exacerbating an already crushing legacy of slavery-based social disabilities, he faces fresh discrimination daily in modern America. In the courts of ten states and the District of Columbia, he is ten times more likely to be imprisoned than his white male counterpart for the same offense. If convicted on a drug charge, he will likely serve a year more in prison than his white male counterpart will for the same charge. While he and his fellow black males constitute 15 percent of the nation's drug users, they make up 33 percent of those arrested for drug use and 57 percent of those convicted. And then they die sooner, and at higher rates of chronic illnesses like AIDS, hypertension, diabetes, cancer, stroke, and Father's killer, heart disease.

Saddest of all, they have no clear understanding of why such debilitating fates have befallen them. There were no clues in their public school education. No guideposts in the popular culture. Theirs was the "now" culture. They felt no impulse to look behind for causes.

The incomparable crime of slavery

Q: What were the five greatest human rights tragedies that occurred in the world over the last five hundred years?

Pose this question to Europeans, Africans, and Americans, and I would guess that you would get dramatically divergent answers.

My guess is that both the Americans and the Europeans would place the Jewish holocaust and [Cambodian leader] Pol Pot's [1970s] extermination of better than a million Cambodians at the top of their list. Perhaps the Europeans would add the Turkish genocide against Armenians. Europe and America would then agree that [Russian-Soviet leader Joseph] Stalin's massive purges [during the 1930s] would qualify him for third, fourth, or fifth place on the list. The Europeans would omit the destruction of Native Americans, in an oversight. The Americans would omit the Native Americans as well, but more for reasons of out-of-sight than oversight. Perhaps one or both would assign fifth place to the 1994 Hutu massacre of Tutsis in Rwanda. No one outside of Africa would remember that from 1890 to 1910 the Belgian King Leopold II (who was viewed at the time in Europe and America as a "philanthropic" monarch) genocidally plundered the Congo, killing as many as ten million people.

Only slavery . . . has hulled empty a whole race of people with inter-generational efficiency.

All of these were unspeakably brutal human rights crimes that occurred over periods ranging from a few weeks to the span of an average lifetime. But in each of these cases, the cultures of those who were killed and persecuted survived the killing spasms. Inasmuch as large numbers, or even remnants of these groups, weathered the savageries with their cultural memories intact, they were able to regenerate themselves and their societies. They rebuilt their places of worship and performed again their traditional religious rituals. They rebuilt their schools and read stories and poems from books written in their traditional languages. They rebuilt stadia, theaters, and amphitheaters in which survivors raised to the heavens in ringing voices songs so old that no one knew when they had been written or who had written them. They remembered their holidays and began to observe them again. They had been trapped on an island in a burning river and many had perished. But the fire had eventually gone out and they could see again their past and future on the river's opposite banks.

The enslavement of black people was practiced in America for 246 years. In spite of and because of its longevity, it would not be placed on the list by either the Americans or the Europeans who had played a central role in slavery's business operations. Yet the black holocaust is far and away the most heinous human rights crime visited upon any group of people in the world over the last five hundred years.

There is oddly no inconsistency here.

Like slavery, other human rights crimes have resulted in the loss of millions of lives. But only slavery, with its sadistic patience, asphyxiated memory, and smothered cultures, has hulled empty a whole race of people with inter-generational efficiency. Every artifact of the victims' past cultures, every custom, every ritual, every god, every language, every trace element of a people's whole hereditary identity, wrenched from them and ground into a sharp choking dust. It is a human rights crime without parallel in the modern world. For it produces its victims *ad infinitum*, long after the active stage of the crime has ended.

A misunderstood tragedy

Our children have no idea who they are. How can we tell them? How can we make them understand who they were before the ocean became a furnace incinerating every pedestal from which the ancient black muses had offered inspiration? What can we say to the black man on death row? The black mother alone, bitter, overburdened, and spent? Who tells them that their fate washed ashore at Jamestown with twenty slaves in 1619?

But Old Massa now, he knows what to say. Like a sexually abusing father with darting snake eyes and liquid lips he whispers—

I know this has hurt and I won't do it again, but don't you tell anybody.

Then on the eve of emancipation, in a wet wheedling voice, Old Massa tells the fucked-up 246-year-old spirit-dead victims with posthypnotic hopefulness—

Now y'all just forget about everything. Gwan now. Gwan.

Go where? Do what? With what? Where is my mother? My father? And theirs? And theirs? I can hear my own voice now loud in my ears.

America has covered itself with a heavy wet material that soaks up annoying complaints like mine. It listens to nothing it does not want to hear and wraps its unread citizens, white and black, in the airless garment of circumambient denial, swathing it all in a lace of fine, sweet lies that further blur everyone's understanding of "why black people are like they are."

America's is a mentality of pictorial information and physical description placed within comprehensible frames of time. We understand tragedy when buildings fall and masses of people die in cataclysmic events. We don't understand tragedy that cannot be quantified arithmetically, requiring more than a gnat's attention span.

6

Reparations Are Not Necessary to Encourage African Americans' Economic Progress

John McWhorter

John McWhorter is the author of Losing the Race: Self-Sabotage in Black America *and a professor of linguistics at the University of California, Berkeley.*

Proponents of slavery reparations contend that the legacy of slavery has forced modern-day African Americans to live in an enduring cycle of poverty. However, the activists' argument for reparations relies on the inaccurate stereotype that "black" most often means "poor" in the United States; in fact, the majority of blacks are enjoying economic success and have entered the middle class. Moreover, since the 1960s, reparations have been provided in the form of welfare and affirmative-action programs. Further handouts will not encourage initiative—the necessary attribute for lasting success—among those blacks who are still struggling below the poverty line.

M y childhood was a typical one for a black American in his mid-thirties. I grew up middle class in a quiet, safe neighborhood in Philadelphia. I still miss living at the top of the tidy little cul-de-sac known as Marion Lane, and to this day there are few things more soothing to me than a walk through Carpenter's Woods across the street.

Blood money

I didn't grow up in a segregated world. My parents didn't live "just enough for the city," as the old Stevie Wonder song goes; my mother taught social work at Temple University and my father was a student ac-

John McWhorter, "Blood Money," *American Enterprise*, vol. 12, July/August 2001, pp. 18–22. Copyright © 2001 by American Enterprise Institute for Public Policy Research. Reproduced by permission of The American Enterprise, a magazine of Politics, Business, and Culture. On the web at www.TAEmag.com.

tivities administrator there. My parents were far from wealthy, living at the edge of their credit cards like many middle class people. But I had everything I needed plus some extras, and spent more time in one of our two cars than on buses.

Contrary to popular belief, I was by no means extraordinarily "lucky" or "unusual" among black Americans of the post–Civil Rights era. There was a time when the childhood I've just described was the province of a tiny "black bourgeoisie." (In 1940, for example, only one in a hundred black families had a middle class income.) But today, there are legions of black adults in the United States who grew up as I did. As a child, I never had trouble finding black peers, and as an adult, meeting black people with life histories like mine requires no searching. In short, in our moment, black success is a norm. Less than one in four black families now live below the poverty line, and the black underclass is at most one out of five blacks. This is what the Civil Rights revolution helped make possible, and I grew up exhilarated at belonging to a race that had made such progress in the face of many obstacles.

Yet today, numerous black officials tell the public that lives like mine are statistical noise, that the overriding situation for blacks is one of penury, dismissal, and spiritual desperation. Under this analysis, the blood of slavery remains on the hands of mainstream America until it allocates a large sum of money to "repair" the unsurmounted damage done to our race over four centuries.

The ideological impulses infecting black America since the mid-1960s make a "reparations" movement not just logical but almost predictable. Yet the notion is a distraction from the real work we have to do.

The shorthand version of the reparations idea is that living blacks are "owed" the money that our slave ancestors were denied for their unpaid servitude. But few black Americans even know the names or life stories of their slave ancestors; almost none of us have pictures or keepsakes from that far back. I am relatively unique even in happening to know my most recent slave ancestor's name—it was also John Hamilton McWhorter. Yes, my slave ancestors were "blood" to me; yes, what was done to them was unthinkable. But the 150 years between me and them has rendered our tie little more than biological. Paying anyone for the suffering of long-dead strangers, even if technically relatives, would be more a matter of blood money than "reparation."

Quite simply, for me to reap a windfall from the first John Hamilton McWhorter's suffering would be a trivialization of his existence. He spent a life in unpaid and permanent servitude; I get paid because every now and then I get trailed by a salesclerk? Or even stopped on a drug check by a policeman? That would dishonor my ancestors' suffering.

False depictions of black poverty

Perhaps recognizing this, the reparations movement is now drifting away from the "back salary" argument to justifications emphasizing the effects of slavery since Emancipation. It is said blacks deserve payment for residual echoes of their earlier disenfranchisement and segregation. This justification, however, is predicated upon the misconception that in 2001, most blacks are "struggling."

This view denies the stunning success that the race has achieved over the past 40 years. It persists because many Americans, black and white, have accepted the leftist notion which arose in the mid-1960s that blacks are primarily victims in this country, that racism and structural injustice hobble all but a few individual blacks. Based on emotion, victimologist thought ignores the facts of contemporary black success and progress, because they do not square with the "blame game."

The depictions of modern black America by reparations advocates—like Randall Robinson, [proreparations activist and] author of *The Debt: What America Owes to Blacks*, who sees nothing but tragedy, scorn, and neglect for blacks in America—often sound even bleaker than analyses by black intellectuals at the turn of the century, when most blacks were still mired in poverty in the South. W.E.B. Du Bois noted back in 1912 that blacks "have in a generation changed from a slave to a free labor system, reestablished family life, accumulated $1,000,000,000 [in] property, including 20,000,000 acres of land, and reduced their illiteracy from 80 to 30 percent."

No valid appeal for reparations can be based on an inaccurate stereotype that "black" means "poor."

One would never hear a modern "civil rights leader" make such a statement today, because it highlights black success rather than failure. This is a serious mistake. No valid appeal for reparations can be based on an inaccurate stereotype that "black" means "poor"—especially when the very people calling for reparations are so quick to decry this stereotype as racist when whites appeal to it.

Reparations cannot logically rely on a depiction of black Americans as a race still reeling from the brutal experience of slavery and its aftereffects. The reality is that, by any estimation, in the year 2001 there are more middle class blacks than poor ones. The large majority of black Americans, while surely not immune to the slings and arrows of the eternal injustices of life on earth, are now leading dignified lives as new variations on what it means to be American.

An argument for reparations that acknowledged the success and basic strength of black America today would aim squarely at the quarter or so of all blacks who are struggling, especially those in the inner cities. Even here, however, we must be careful about what "reparations" would be intended to do. If all black Americans living below the poverty line were given a subsidy to move to the suburbs, free tuition for college, and/or a small business loan, all indications are that it would make no difference in the overall condition of most of their lives in the long run. As the pitfalls of [low-income housing assistance] Section 8 programs in various cities have shown, a house in the suburbs cannot undo deeply ingrained cultural patterns etched by racism of the past but today self-generating.

Money to attend college is of little use in a culture that has inherited from the Black Power movement a tendency to equate scholarly commitment (beyond black-related topics) with "acting white." This pulls down the performance of even many middle class black students. The less privileged ones too often just drop out entirely.

The person who obtains a small business loan on his own can't help but have a deeper commitment to its success than the person who is simply handed a check from on high with no questions asked. This has been painfully clear from the checkered and often corrupt record of minority businesses that owe their existence to contracts meted out according to racial preferences.

Individual initiative over handouts

The reality is that the only way for any group of human beings to succeed is through individual initiative. This may not be fair for a group with a history of oppression, but history records no other pathway to the top. In the mid-1960s, America experimented with the idea, a reasonable guess on its face, that simply giving handouts to poor blacks would enable them to bypass the conventional route to self-realization. But today the data are in: a three-generations-deep welfare culture where work was an option rather than a given, where a passive and victimhood-based relationship to mainstream accomplishment was endemic. There is nothing "black" about this, given that similar policies have left an equally bleak situation in Native American communities, as well as white ones in Appalachia.

Any effort to repair problems in black America must focus on helping people to help themselves.

A "reparations" movement predicated upon the fiction that more brute handouts will raise large numbers of black people out of poverty would actually work against true and lasting uplift, leaving life nasty, brutish, and short for millions of black people. As the old adage goes—one which many blacks would spontaneously applaud—"Give a man a fish and he'll eat for a day, teach a man to fish and he'll eat forever."

Any effort to repair problems in black America must focus on helping people to help themselves. Funds must be devoted to ushering welfare mothers into working for a living, so that their children do not grow up learning that employment is something "other people" do. Inner city communities should be helped to rebuild themselves, in part through making it easier for residents to buy their homes. Police forces ought to be trained to avoid brutality, which turns young blacks against the mainstream today, and to work with, rather than against, the communities they serve.

Finally, this country must support all possible efforts to liberate black children from the soul-extinguishing influence of ossified urban public schools, and to move them into experimental or all-minority schools where a culture of competition is fostered. This will help undo the sense that intellectual excellence is a "white" endeavor. Surely we must improve the public schools as well, including increasing the exposure of young black children to standardized tests. But we also must make sure another generation of black children are not lost during the years it will take for these schools to get their acts together.

Most readers will have noticed that all of the things I just described are in fact taking place. [President] George W. Bush's Faith-Based and Community Initiatives[1] effort is a long-overdue attempt to bring black churches into play in helping make innercity neighborhoods stable communities. Meanwhile, community development corporations are slowly working quiet wonders in such neighborhoods by granting inner-city people loans with which to purchase real estate. The [1977] Community Reinvestment Act concurrently spurs banks to make small business loans to minorities.

Numerous cities are demonstrating that cooperation between police forces and minority communities can lead to massive drops in crime. And the Bush administration is pressing to move minority children into functioning schools, while advocating increased testing of all students (though the Democrats' coddling of teachers' unions in return for votes presents a mighty obstacle).

In other words, it could be argued that America is already in the business of "reparations" for blacks, teaching us to fish instead of just giving us a dinner wrapped in newspaper.

Welfare "reparations"

Furthermore, there have already been what any outside observer would term "reparations" since the 1960s. When reparations fans grouse that "It's time America acknowledged slavery," one wonders just what they thought the "War on Poverty" [enacted by President Lyndon Johnson in the mid-1960s] was. In the 1930s, welfare policies were primarily intended for widows. In the mid-1960s, welfare programs were deliberately expanded for the "benefit" of black people.

Federal and state governments have since poured billions of dollars into welfare payments and the imposing bureaucracy that grew up along with them. This very bureaucracy has gone on to provide secure government jobs for several million blacks. The byzantine industry of urban social service agencies familiar to us today did not exist before the late 1960s.

Despite [antipoverty programs], . . . the sentiment persists among certain blacks that America somehow "owes" us still.

None of this was specifically termed "reparations," but it certainly provided unearned cash for underclass blacks for decades, as well as sinecure jobs for a great many others. Today, welfare programs are thankfully being recast as temporary stopgaps, with welfare mothers being trained for work. The funds and efforts devoted to this laudable effort are again a concrete attempt to overcome structural poverty. A society with no commitment to addressing the injustices of the past wouldn't bother with any of this effort aimed at poor blacks.

---

1. George W. Bush's Faith-Based and Community Initiatives are proposals to use taxpayer revenues to support charity-run welfare programs.

Affirmative action policies were similarly developed to acknowledge earlier slights. Initially intended as a call to recruit qualified blacks for hiring or school admission, the policy quickly transmogrified into quota systems, with lesser qualified blacks all too often being given positions over better qualified whites. Even most blacks under about age 45 tend to tacitly think of affirmative action as a "reparation," although they would not put it in just that way.

Ultimately, a race shows its worth . . . in how well it can do in the absence of charity.

Despite the Herculean efforts we have seen over the past few decades, the sentiment persists among certain blacks that America somehow "owes" us still. These reparations advocates are at heart motivated by a broken self-image, a deepseated insecurity about being black. This renders cries of victimhood imperative, because they are internally soothing. Black success is "beside the point" until all whites avidly "like" us. This is what blinds reparations advocates to the fact that most whites—especially educated and influential ones—long ago heard the message. It was Peter Edelman who resigned from the Clinton administration's Department of Health and Human Services over the reform of the welfare laws, and white former university presidents William Bowen [Princeton University] and Derek Bok [Harvard University] who penned the most prominent book-length defense of affirmative action, *The Shape of the River.*

Because the reparations movement is ultimately based on an inferiority complex rather than empirical engagement, the only "reparations" acceptable to its advocates would have to be officially titled as such, granted by a white America explicitly designating itself as the agent of all black misery past and present.

The harm of reparations

The problem is that no aid package could possibly have any substantial or lasting effect on black America unless it is designed to elicit self-generated initiative. And such packages are already in operation, though not titled as "reparations." Teaching disadvantaged blacks how to fish is exactly what the reform of welfare [time limits on benefits were imposed in 1996], the Office of Faith-Based and Community Initiatives, the community development corporations, the Community Reinvestment Act, the school voucher movement, and even the gradual rollback of racial preferences are all designed to do. A package of new handouts and set-asides, tied in a ribbon as a sop to black leaders' addiction to the giveaways of condescending white leftists, would not only have no serious benefit, it would do outright harm.

There would be damage on both sides of the racial divide. As the magic transformations of the package inevitably failed to appear, the flop would be attributed to there not having been enough money granted. Next a new mantra would become established in the black community to cover the bitter disappointment: "They think they can treat us like animals for four hundred years and then just pay us off?" Meanwhile, non-blacks would begin to grouse "They got reparations—what are they still complaining about?" Whether these mutterings would be valid is beside the point, what matters is that they would arise and be passed on to a new generation, to further poison interracial relations in this country.

Ultimately, a race shows its worth not by how much charity it can extract from others, but in how well it can do in the absence of charity. Black America has elicited more charity from its former oppressors than any race in human history—justifiably in my view. However, this can only serve as a spark—the real work is now ours.

The only reparations I could live with are the substantial ones already in effect, which show all signs of making a difference to the minority of blacks left behind during the explosion of the black middle class. There are certainly some additional steps that could be taken to improve the chances of the black underclass: increased child-care centers to make it easier for inner-city mothers to work; better transportation from cities to suburbs to make it easier to get to places of employment; more research on and funding for drug rehabilitation. There would be no harm in labeling a package of policies of this sort "reparations."

But in the end, most reparations activists would see this as "not enough": The reforms I've described are designed for the mundane business of concrete and measurable uplift. What most reparations advocates are seeking, on the other hand, is an emotional balm: a comprehensive mea culpa by white America of responsibility for everything that ails any blacks.

This version of "civil rights," however, is a mere excrescence of our moment—a competition for eliciting pity, which pre-1960s civil-rights leaders would barely recognize. And it will pass.

7

African American Poverty Should Be Addressed Without Resorting to Reparations

Wendy Kaminer

Wendy Kaminer is a senior correspondent for the liberal political magazine the American Prospect *and is a contributing editor at the* Atlantic Monthly. *She also serves on the national board of the American Civil Liberties Union, a legal organization that defends free speech and individual rights.*

Calls for slavery reparations are based on the assertion that the institution of slavery and the era of racism that followed it have led to widespread African American poverty. The problem with the appeal for reparations is that it relies on a belief in the justice of inherited guilt—that in order to achieve equality in the present, Americans whose families had nothing to do with slavery should pay for the sins of centuries-dead slaveholders. Equality for African Americans should not be justified by appeals to right past wrongs nor should it be "purchased" with the sufferings of one's ancestors. The inherited poverty of African Americans should be remedied directly through public education, health care, and transportation programs. Such programs should be pursued not in the spirit of righting past wrongs but in paving the way for the future.

Self invention has always been an American ideal. We're supposed to enjoy opportunities to make our own fortunes and control our own fates, in this world and the next. The Calvinism of seventeenth-century colonials proved less quintessentially American than did the notion that you can choose to be born again in Christ. This is not a culture inclined to embrace ideas of predestination, spiritual or financial. In the mythic, utterly egalitarian America—the democratic America [French historian Alexis de] Tocqueville described—we create our own futures, unburdened by our familial pasts.

Reparations and inherited guilt

That is the American dream and a primary ideological obstacle to winning reparations for slavery.

Demands for reparations challenge the vision of an American meritocracy. African Americans have not enjoyed equal opportunities for self invention, advocates of reparations insist: Tenacious economic discrimination, widespread denials of voting rights, and oppressive brutalities, (like lynching) followed the abolition of slavery and made sure that the descendants of slaves would be burdened by their history, not freed from it.

I don't dispute the truth of this assertion; the persistence of discrimination throughout the twentieth century is a primary justification for affirmative action, which I have always supported, a little unhappily. Race-conscious hiring, promotion, and admission policies are not entirely equitable, but they are necessary and, on balance, less inequitable than race-blind policies. Still I don't regard affirmative action as compensation for the past; I regard it as insurance for the future. I don't support affirmative action programs because I believe that white women and racial minorities have somehow earned the right to preferential treatment, by inadvertently inheriting discrimination. I support affirmative action because I can't figure out a better way to achieve equality.

Reparations for slavery should have been paid in the late 1800s, when they were first demanded.

So I hesitate to endorse recent demands for slavery reparations, although they have been thoughtfully presented. Opening a new conversation about reparations, activists and intellectuals, like Randall Robinson [author of *The Debt: What America Owes to Blacks*] and [Harvard University law professor] Charles Ogletree, have stressed that they are not asking for direct cash payments to African Americans; reparations may take the form of compensatory social and economic programs. (In a March 2000 article in *The Nation*, Robinson called for "public initiatives, not personal checks.") They have not accused those Americans whose ancestors were not enslaved of collaborating in the perpetuation of racism. "No one holds any living person responsible for slavery" or its legacies, Robinson stressed. They have made an appeal to our collective conscience, not issued an indictment of collective guilt.

Still, it's hard to imagine how this appeal might be implemented more than 100 years after abolition, without encouraging a belief in inherited guilt. Reparation demands do rest on the conviction that the nation owes a debt to its black citizens. This view implicitly implicates all citizens who constitute the nation, except the victims of slavery. First-, second-, or third-generation Americans whose families were busy being persecuted in some other country when slavery was abolished here may be particularly resistant to the demand that they contribute to reparations, but even if you don't believe in inherited guilt, it's difficult to make a case against the descendants of slaveholders.

How will we identify the beneficiaries of reparations? Will they be limited to people of African ancestry? Will they include those Americans of African descent whose ancestors participated in the slave trade? Will they include all those Americans of mixed race descended from slaves and slaveholders? If reparations are intended to atone for racism, will they extend to all self identified people of color, like Hispanics, Native Americans, or Pacific Islanders? Will the drive for reparations provoke a close examination of our ancestry to determine racial purity and entitlement to compensation?

Irremediable history

Irritating questions like these are sure to follow from demands for reparations. They illustrate the difficulties of atoning for sins committed over a century ago. The perpetrators and their victims have been dead for generations, and we can't identify their survivors, which makes the payment of slavery reparations much more complicated and controversial than the compensation of Jewish Holocaust victims, Japanese citizens interned during World War II, or blacks who witnessed the murderous riots in Greenwood, Oklahoma, in the 1920s. [Hundreds of blacks were murdered by white mobs in the Greenwood section of Tulsa, Oklahoma, in 1921.] (A 1997 commission in Oklahoma recommended that reparations be paid to the survivors of the Greenwood massacre.)[1] Reparations for slavery should have been paid in the late 1800s, when they were first demanded, or at least in the early 1900s. It's not fair, but it may be inevitable that the failure to recognize claims for compensation within a generation or two makes them virtually impossible to recognize at all.

We shouldn't have to rationalize efforts to achieve [equality] by labeling those efforts compensation for the past.

I'm not offering this as an excuse for amnesia about our history, but the difficulties of designing reparations do suggest that history is sometimes irremediable. I am always nonplussed and a little annoyed when some head of state offers an apology for the crimes of his predecessors. While I understand the symbolic value of Tony Blair's apology to the Irish or Clinton's apology to Africa for the U.S. role in slavery, I still find their contrition rather cloying. It's easy to atone for someone else's sins. Vicarious apologies are cheap thrills for the sanctimonious.

This does not condemn us to inaction when we are confronted with racism and economic inequities in the present. I might support many of the public initiatives offered by advocates for reparations, but I'd justify them differently. Why must we suggest that, by accidents of birth, people have somehow earned the right to government assistance in achieving equality?

There's an ideological paradox at the heart of demands for reparations:

---

1. In June 2001, Oklahoma governor Frank Keating authorized full-tuition scholarships for three hundred Tulsa residents.

They challenge the myth of an American meritocracy, as the civil rights movement once challenged the myth of legal equality. Reparations aim to make the meritocratic ideal a reality for African Americans, as the civil rights movement aimed to realize the constitutional ideal of equality under law. But the campaign for reparations also reflects some of the premises of the aristocracy it attacks: It allows the past to define our entitlements in the present; it relies on a belief in the justice of inheritance.

If equality is an American birthright, we shouldn't have to rationalize efforts to achieve it by labeling those efforts compensation for the past. Whether or not your great-great-grandparents were enslaved, you ought not to be consigned to substandard schools, excluded from home ownership by discriminatory lending or sales practices, or subject to arbitrary searches by police because of the color of your skin. If equality is a birthright, you don't have to purchase it with the sufferings of your ancestors, any more than you should be allowed to purchase privileges with your ancestors' achievements.

Reparations do not address poverty directly

It's a coincidence worth noting that demands for reparations have followed a drive to reduce or even eliminate estate taxes and allow for tax-free transfers of wealth between generations. [President] George W. Bush, who essentially inherited his place at Yale University . . . , opposes the "death tax." I suspect that like many aristocrats, including [former U.S. vice president] Al Gore, Bush feels deserving of the privileges he's inherited. I suspect he is irrationally proud of what he considers to be the accomplishments of his father and grandfather (accomplishments for which he can claim no credit); maybe he's proud of his "bloodlines."

I have no quarrel with noblesse oblige (it helped shape [U.S. president] Franklin D. Roosevelt). But noblesse oblige reflects a commitment to making yourself worthy of what you've inherited, a commitment to earning your privilege with your own labors—not justifying it with the labors of your forebears. Bush, for one, doesn't exhibit noblesse oblige; he exhibits a sense of inherited entitlement, which is echoed in campaigns for reparations.

Underlying the demand for reparations is one of the great taboos of American politics: the demand for redistribution of wealth. The compensatory programs envisioned by reparations advocates are essentially redistributive; they're intended to raise the economic status of blacks. As Robinson suggests, they would acknowledge and undo the "mechanisms" that have pushed blacks to "the back of the line." But if the problem is a system of inherited poverty and inherited wealth, why not address it directly?

If I were queen, just before abolishing my office, I'd raise taxes on intergenerational transfers of wealth and use the proceeds to help build a meritocracy. Maybe I'd devote the additional revenues to public education, health care, or transportation. Maybe I'd compensate people victimized by racial profiling. Maybe I'd fund some of the public initiatives proposed by Robinson, but I wouldn't call them reparations. We shouldn't have to justify equality.

8

Reparations Lawsuits Will Rectify the Injustice of Slavery

Vincene Verdun

Vincene Verdun is an associate professor of law and African American studies at Ohio State University in Columbus.

Lawsuits filed in 2002 are seeking damages from corporations who profited from slavery in the United States. Critics of these suits argue that too many years have passed since the end of slavery and therefore these suits should be barred by the statute of limitations. Resistance to such lawsuits also centers around the fact that no slaves are alive to compensate. However, corporations, abetted by the federal government, contributed to African American poverty by openly practicing racial discrimination for decades after the end of slavery. Therefore, it is reasonable to hold corporations liable for reparations, and the statute of limitations should not apply.

Lawsuits were filed [in March 2002] in federal district courts in New York and New Jersey on behalf of [attorney and prominent reparations activist] Deadria Farmer-Paellman and Richard E. Barber as representatives of slave descendants against corporations involved in slavery. The suits seek an accounting of slavery-related profits and damages based on unjust enrichment.

Bypassing the statute of limitations

It is hard to argue that profits derived from slavery were not unjustly earned, or that it is inappropriate to have these corporations share in repairing the broken lives of those who suffer most from slavery's legacy. For example, who cares to argue that corporate profits derived from the use of Jewish slave labor during the Holocaust were not unjustly earned?

I agree that no slave masters are alive to pay the debt of slavery in America. However, the government, as a body corporate that supported slavery and systematic discrimination, is still around.

The many corporations that built fortunes through the slave trade are still around. These corporate bodies, although not slave masters per se, were perpetrators in crimes against humanity, and some portion of the wealth that makes up their bottom lines is the product of slave labor.

Given the egregious impact of slavery and discrimination, the statute of limitations [on reparations suits] should, equitably, be tolled.

Some argue that the legal case for reparations is barred by the statute of limitations and other procedural hurdles. But let's take a new perspective on time. If all had been fair and equal at the end of slavery, if freedmen had enjoyed equal opportunity and equal protection of the law in the absence of discrimination, there would be a strong case that it is too late to seek reparations for slavery.

Unfortunately, the history of the United States is not so rosy and provides a contrary story. We must ask, "When is it too late to redress a longstanding wrong that continues?" Until the civil rights revolution and affirmative action, only the most fortunate African-Americans had any semblance of a chance to share in the prosperity of this nation.

Academic institutions and corporations opened the doors of opportunity to African-Americans around 1969. If we use that year as the trigger date for the statute of limitations, only 33 years have passed. Evidence of the nature of the true perpetrators, such as the corporations involved, surfaced only recently. Given the egregious impact of slavery and discrimination, the statute of limitations should, equitably, be tolled.

Crimes against humanity

The 2001 World Conference Against Racism in Durban, South Africa, labeled slavery a crime against humanity. Poverty is defined by the United Nations Committee on Human Rights not only as a lack of physical resources, but as deprivation of economic, political and social rights. The message is clear: Slavery begat racism begat poverty and exclusion; reparations are the way to rectify these injustices.

The United States vigorously resists the idea of reparations for slavery. That comes as no surprise.

Slavery was protected by the U.S. Constitution, despite its obvious incompatibility with the Declaration of Independence. When slavery was formally eliminated with the 13th, 14th and 15th amendments to the Constitution after the Civil War, it was replaced with Black Codes [Southern laws restricting the civil rights of blacks], sharecropping, discrimination and oppression that included systematic failure of the government to recognize and protect the rights of African-Americans, even as newly freed slaves.

Let's not forget *Plessy v. Ferguson* [an 1896 Supreme Court decision], which condoned segregation. Congress failed to enact lynch laws despite the fact that more than 10,000 freedmen were lynched between 1865 and

1895. The federal government practiced systematic discrimination in the armed services, farm loans, home mortgages and many federal programs.

Resistance to reparations is frequently based on standing issues: There are no slaves alive to compensate. At the same time, though, no one can reasonably argue that the impact of slavery is not being experienced by African-Americans today. Slavery was doctrinally supported by racism and the effects of that racism are felt in the lives of African-Americans without regard to their economic, social and political stature.

Of course, the magnitude of the impact of slavery and its aftermath is significantly more pronounced in lives of those people also caught in the web of poverty. Racism-induced poverty is not likely to disappear of its own accord. In the abstract, procedural defenses to reparations, such as standing and the statute of limitations, are flimsy at best. Given the magnitude of slavery and the impact it has had on the lives of African-Americans, procedural defenses are downright cowardly.

9

Reparations Lawsuits Face Numerous Legal Hurdles

Allen C. Guelzo

Allen C. Guelzo is dean of the Templeton Honors College at Eastern University in St. David's, Pennsylvania, and is the author of Abraham Lincoln: Redeemer President.

Reparations payments made to Jewish survivors of the Holocaust and to Japanese Americans for their internment during World War II are cited as legal precedents by proponents of slavery reparations for African Americans. The federal government, however, cannot be held liable for slavery because slavery was legalized by state, not federal, statutes. In addition, too many years have passed to hold corporations involved in the slave trade accountable. Identifying who should receive reparations would be even more difficult since much racial mixing has occured since the Civil War. The Civil War itself should be considered the ultimate "mechanism of justice" paid to African Americans for slavery.

On May 4, 1969, James Forman rose to interrupt the Sunday morning services at New York City's Riverside Church to read aloud a "Black Manifesto." The Manifesto was an explosive declaration of independence by a new generation of young black activists who had grown impatient with the slow-moving, nonviolent tactics that had prevailed in the Civil Rights Movement. It was intended to shock, and shock it did, not least because, among its other features, it demanded $500 million as reparations "due us as a people who have been exploited and degraded, brutalized, killed, and persecuted."

Holocaust survivors redefine reparations

The idea that one party to a conflict can end up owing financial reparations in some form or other to the opposing party is not a new one. The most notorious example is the reparation imposed by the Allied Powers at the end of World War I on Germany by the Versailles Treaty. But the war reparations of Versailles belonged to a very different category from the reparations Forman was demanding. In 1921, reparations were based on the damages inflicted by outright war, not social or political wrongs, and they were imposed by the winners on the losers. In other words, it was the victims who paid reparations, not the victimizers. What made Forman's demand possible in 1969 was an important redefinition of the idea of reparations that grew out of the experience of World War II and the discovery of the extermination of six million of Europe's Jews by the Nazis.

Fundamental problems that did not exist in [other reparations] cases stand in the way of slave reparations.

As early as 1943, the World Jewish Congress had begun to formulate demands for a postwar settlement that would include restoration or indemnity for stolen or destroyed Jewish property, reparations for the loss of Jewish life and community that included payments of up to $12 billion, and guarantees from the Allies for a Jewish homeland in Palestine. What raised eyebrows about these demands was not their size but the fact that they came from an ethnic group, rather than a nation or state, and a group which was asking that its ethnic identity become the basis for the reparations. This was so unprecedented that the 1945 Paris Conference on Reparations chose to ignore the Jewish demands. However, in 1951, German Chancellor Konrad Adenauer, who viewed Jewish reparations as part of the burden Germans needed to confront frankly in order to wipe out the Nazi past, offered reparations amounting to DM [Deutschmarks] 3.45 billion to the survivors of the Holocaust, and a second agreement in 1953 committed the Federal Republic to still further reparations payments.

The success of the Jewish survivors of the Holocaust in gaining reparations was a turning point in the notion of reparations for national crimes. It not only reversed the conventional direction of reparations, but it legitimized demands for reparations for past injustices by groups who had no specific national identity of their own. In 1962, Australian Aborigines filed a suit against the Australian federal government for the recovery of traditional tribal lands. An Aboriginal Land Act was passed in 1976, and in 1998 Australia celebrated (if that is the word) an official Sorry Day for Aborigines as a way of offering a national apology. In 1997, the World Jewish Congress succeeded in exposing the complicity of the Swiss banking system with the Nazi persecution of German Jews, and, after some hesitation, Swiss banks announced their intention to create a Holocaust Fund for Holocaust victims whose family assets had disappeared into Nazi accounts in Swiss banks.

Slave reparations and individual harm

The United States first became involved in the new wave of reparations in 1988, when Congress passed the Civil Liberties Act, allowing the federal government to compensate Japanese-Americans who had been interned during the Second World War. But the most obvious candidate for reparations, as James Forman had foreseen in 1969, would be the descendants of the African-Americans who, from 1619 until 1865, had been legally enslaved in the United States. Few people took Forman seriously in 1969, but as money began to flow to Holocaust survivors and Japanese-American internees, it became difficult for African-Americans not to wonder bitterly why they should be denied a place at the reparations table. In 1989, Michigan representative John Conyers introduced a bill (H.R. 3745) asking for the establishment of a commission "to examine the institution of slavery" and "to make recommendations to the Congress on appropriate remedies."

Conyers' bill was buried in the House Judiciary Committee for several years. [As of 2003, Conyers' bill remains in congressional committee.] But it was reintroduced in 1993 as H.R. 40 with forty-eight sponsors and the blessing of the Congressional Black Caucus. Then, in December 2000, Charles Ogletree of the Harvard University Law School formed a Reparations Coordinating Committee (originally known as the Reparations Assessment Group) composed of several high-profile veterans of national class-action lawsuits, including Johnnie Cochran, Richard Scruggs, and Dennis Sweet . . . , who began exploring the possibility of litigation to obtain reparations.

But if the Japanese and Swiss examples offered an incentive for demanding the reparations Forman described, they did not offer much in the way of useful guidance, since three fundamental problems that did not exist in the Jewish or Japanese cases stand in the way of slave reparations.

It will be hard to win a civil lawsuit brought against the heirs of [slaveholders] who [were] . . . merely operating under the laws of the time.

First, American law, both in terms of statute law and common law, is rooted in long historical assumptions about where rights are located. From the time of the American founding, we have understood rights to be located in individuals. We recognize no titles of nobility: this means not only that the American republic repudiates the notion of a titled aristocracy, but that it does not recognize any special category of rights belonging to a class of people. There is, in the politics of the Founders, no essential quality of nobility that all aristocrats are presumed to share and others not, and which we are all obliged to recognize legally. By the same logic, we recognize no national language, no national church, and no national race, because we do not locate civil status or rights in groups, whether those groups are ethnic, religious, or racial. So, when a crime is committed, we want to know about the guilt or innocence of the individual, not someone's racial group, religion, or other characteristic. And when a civil judgment is issued, we want to compensate the individuals who were actually harmed, even in a class action, not the race or church or bowling league they belong to.

The grain of American jurisprudence thus runs completely against assigning blame on the basis of group identity (something which we have shown most recently in our instinctive recoil from the practice of racial profiling). It expresses the measure of resistance we have toward identifying individuals as anything but individuals, and it poses a philosophical stumbling block for reparations litigation right on the threshold of the courtroom.

A question of tactics

But this only speaks to a general conceptual issue. There are two other equally difficult problems standing in the way of reparations for slavery that were not present in the other reparations cases.

For one thing, what tactics should reparations activists adopt? Advocates like Charles Ogletree hope to use civil litigation, through the sort of class-action lawsuits that won such immense victories as the tobacco settlement. On March 26, 2002, a group of New York–based lawyers headed by Edward D. Fagan, who spearheaded successful suits on behalf of Holocaust survivors against European firms that collaborated with the Nazis in using concentration camp inmates as laborers, filed suit in U.S. District Court in Brooklyn against Fleets-Boston Financial, the insurance giant Aetna, and railroad conglomerate CSX Corporation, on the grounds that these corporations are the successors of companies that profited from slavery before the Civil War. The defendants, claims Fagan's suit, "conspired with slave traders, with each other and other entities and institutions . . . to commit and/or knowingly facilitate crimes against humanity, and to further illicitly profit from slave labor." Ogletree and Cochran have promised to file similar suits against other corporate targets and the United States government. . . .

> *The difficulty in identifying whom we might sue for reparations . . . pales beside the difficulty of identifying who the beneficiaries ought to be.*

The success of the Holocaust and tobacco settlements has given this kind of litigation a sort of cachet in the public view. Outside the public gaze, however, the truth is that litigation has not been terribly successful in gaining ground for reparations. In 1995, a reparations lawsuit demanding $100 million was filed against the federal government in the Ninth Circuit Court of Appeals. But the suit, *Cato v. United States*, was tossed out on the grounds that it lacked a "legally cognizable basis." And no wonder: the statutes that made slavery legal were state, not federal statutes, and thus do not render the federal government liable for slavery. After all, the Constitution nowhere contains the word slave, an omission that the late Don E. Fehrenbacher suspected was a deliberate tactic of the authors of the Constitution to keep the federal government from having jurisdiction, or responsibility, for slavery. And besides, the federal government possesses sovereign immunity [a legal doctrine that precludes a lawsuit against a government without its consent]; only if Congress agreed to surrender that immunity beforehand could a class-action suit ever hope to gain a victory through the federal appeals system.

One could turn, in that case, to suing the states that legalized slavery, since that is where the legal center of enslavement rested. The problem here is that the plaintiffs in any such suit would be obliged to sue not only the states we think of as having been slaveholding states—the states of the old Confederacy—but any state where slavery had been legalized at any time. That would include Massachusetts, New York, Pennsylvania, and Illinois. The idea of suing Pennsylvania, which voluntarily abolished slavery in 1780, or any other Northern state like it, stretches public credulity. Attorneys-general in those states would unquestionably fight any such suit, and the likelihood of failure in those state courts would cast a shadow over litigation in the others.

Targeting the descendants of slaveowners and corporations

Instead of suits against the one-time slave states, one could turn to the descendants of the owners of slaves, and sue them. As Edward Ball demonstrated in his best-selling [1998 book] *Slaves in the Family*, it is not impossible to trace back the family trees of slaves and slaveowners in place after place, with the aid of census records, tax records, and probate records, and identify who exactly was guilty of enslaving whom. Not impossible, but not easy. In the first place, it will be hard to win a civil lawsuit brought against the heirs of anyone who was, before 1861, merely operating under the laws of the time. Second, it will be a challenge to calibrate the exact amount of the guilt slaveholding involved for different individuals. At one point or other, perhaps half of Southern whites owned at least one slave at some time, and a third were long-term slaveholders. It will take painstaking research to determine how much liability adheres to a family that might have owned one or two slaves at different times over two hundred years, and how much to a family that owned hundreds of slaves without interruption, and under conditions that would make any civilized conscience falter. This also assumes that the wealth a family's slaves generated for it is still attachable in some form. More likely, any assets a family once possessed through the labor of its slaves have long since disappeared.

The last real hope of reparations litigation is to target corporations, in the way that the March 26, 2002, suit has done, and which Ogletree threatens to do. Once again, there is a certain verisimilitude to the charge that as many as one thousand modern corporations were involved, a century and a half ago, in one or another aspect of bondage. A number of modern urban newspapers, such as the *Baltimore Sun*, the *Richmond Times-Dispatch*, and the *Hartford Courant* ran advertisements before the Civil War for the sale of slaves or the recapture of runaways; all four of the major North American railroads own rail lines that were built with slave labor; the founder of Lehman Brothers [a global investment bank] bought slaves as workers for the firm when it was founded in pre–Civil War Alabama. But even here, the odds for legal success remain long. None of these businesses survive in the same organizational state as 150 years ago; some of the names are only historical reminders, left after a century of mergers and acquisitions; and many of them have already put into place elaborate affirmative hiring policies, racial sensitivity training, and programs that underwrite black education.

But if they are not all that vulnerable legally to reparations demands, corporations are vulnerable in other ways. Corporations have products; they also have reputations that sell those products, and even an unsuccessful lawsuit can have damaging impact on the corporation's image and sales. In a major *USA Today* series of articles on reparations, Owen Pell, a lawyer who represented Chase Manhattan Bank against claims made by Holocaust survivors, acknowledged that corporations would rather settle high-emotion, high-visibility suits like those planned by the Reparations Coordinating Committee in some quiet, out-of-court fashion. "Companies have learned you don't judge a lawsuit by its merits," Pell commented. "You judge it by the potential public relations damage." This may, in the end, be the most successful way to use litigation to get reparations promises from anxious corporate executives. But those who rely on this sort of legal bluff will have a public relations problem of their own, since it will be difficult for them to pose as champions of justice in the middle of what looks like just another Jesse Jackson [controversial civil rights leader]–style shakedown. And there is no guarantee that unsympathetic shareholders might not vent their own outrage with countersuits against the same quailing executives.

Identifying beneficiaries is problematic

The difficulty in identifying whom we might sue for reparations is considerable. But it pales beside the difficulty of identifying who the beneficiaries ought to be. This is what decisively distances the Japanese internees and the Holocaust survivors from the slave reparations question, because in the first two cases there were identifiable individuals to whom benefits, restitution, and indemnity could be paid. But American slavery ended 137 years ago [1865], and at the farthest stretch, only a handful of the grandchildren of those slaves might possibly be alive today. This, of course, is where the notion of group identity enters into the reparations argument, since the crime of slavery—by the logic of modern reparations—was committed, not against individuals, but against a group (African-Americans) and therefore reparations can be paid to a group (African-American descendants).

But that will only be the case if we are able, indeed, to identify such a group with any accuracy. And that may not be so obvious as it seems. The long record of racial mixing under slavery between masters and female slaves (as in the much-debated case of Thomas Jefferson and Sally Hemings) produced populations that were so lightskinned that they passed into white society (as several of Sally Hemings' children did) and populations so darkskinned that they lost all memory of the white European genes they inherited. If the group to be identified as the recipients of reparations payments is simply to be "African-Americans," then there will be a surprising number of claimants eligible for reparations payments who have, so to speak, been "white" for several generations.[1] By the same token, if the object of reparations litigation is to be the descendants of

1. This is precisely what happened when the Mohegan and Pequot [Native American] tribes of Connecticut opened casinos on tribal territory in the mid-1990s and proposed to distribute the considerable profits of the casinos to the members of their tribes. "When word got out that being a Pequot was worth a great deal of money," drily commented Scott Malcolmson in *One Drop of Blood: The American Misadventure of Race*, "ancestral memories were rekindled," or in some cases manufactured, to get a share of the boodle.

slave-owners, what do we do when many of those who sue are themselves descendants of those same slave-owners, and also belong, by reasons of racial mixing, to the class of those being sued?

The calls for reparations are ignoring the ways in which reparations have already been paid and are being paid.

Rather than litigation, it has been suggested that reparations activists pursue a legislative agenda, since time after time this has proven to be a more successful strategy. In the 1980s, the Japanese American Citizens League, in its quest for reparations for the World War II–era detention of Japanese-Americans, resisted the temptation to challenge the federal government in court, and instead lobbied Congress to form a nonpartisan fact-finding commission. The commission's hearings then became a rallying point for publicizing Japanese-American sufferings during the internment, while the commission's independent status allowed its findings and recommendations for reparations to appear nonpartisan. And the result was a substantial victory for the families of the internees. Not surprisingly, this is the route that Conyers and his supporters have chosen to follow.

There is a certain chanciness in this tactic, however, in that a legislative commission can only recommend certain results to a legislature, not mandate them. Unlike in the civil courts, a victory in Congress does not necessarily result in an award for damages. Congress, for instance, could very easily have received the report of the internees commission and merely issued an apology that would have closed the door for good on further civil litigation, and the same could very easily happen concerning reparations for slavery. What is just as likely is that a commission will deadlock, and issue no recommendations at all. One of the most hopeful examples of using independent commissions to get around political roadblocks, the Kerrey Commission on entitlements, was loaded with blue-ribbon experts—Senators, bankers, philanthropists, college presidents. But when it issued its report in 1995, the membership couldn't even agree on what the problem was, much less how to fix it. Reparations activists consequently run the risk of conjuring up all kinds of irritations in commission testimony, without any guarantee of a substantive result.

The Civil War as a "mechanism of justice"

Those irritations could arise especially if it appears that the calls for reparations are ignoring the ways in which reparations have already been paid and are being paid. Affirmative action is, for instance, a form of reparations, and it ill-behooves advocates for reparations to appear dismissive of an initiative that has cost more than a little controversy. But I am thinking of another form of reparations for slavery that Americans have paid, and that is what brings me at last to Abraham Lincoln [U.S. president 1861–65].

Lincoln knew as well as any American of his time what the injustices of slavery involved. To a delegation of black leaders in 1862, he admitted candidly that "I think your race suffer very greatly. . . . Your race are suffering, in my judgment, the greatest wrong inflicted on any people." But Lincoln's notion of the debt created by this injustice was balanced by the kind of payment he saw being made in the carnage of the Civil War. "If I had been allowed my way this war would have been ended before this," he wrote to the English Quaker Eliza P. Gurney in the fall of 1862, but God "permits it for some wise purpose of His own." Lincoln thought, by 1865, that he could discern that purpose, and the purpose was the payment of reparations in a dearer currency than money could calculate.

In his Second Inaugural, little more than a month before his death, Lincoln reminded the nation of the dread warning given to those who had oppressed the innocent and defenseless: Woe unto the world because of offenses; for it must needs be that offenses come, but woe to that man by whom the offense cometh. From that biblical lesson, Lincoln asked whether such a woe had indeed come on the nation because of slavery—and was being paid for in blood. "If we shall suppose that American slavery is one of those offenses which, in the providence of God, must needs come, but which, having continued through His appointed time, He now wills to remove, and that He gives to both North and South this terrible war as the woe due to those by whom the offense came," Lincoln continued, then what other sense can this war have, except that God has willed that the war should be a mechanism of justice, "until all the wealth piled by the bondsman's two hundred and fifty years of unrequited toil shall be sunk, and until every drop of blood drawn with the lash shall be paid by another drawn with the sword"?

Those for whom this way of paying reparations was not justice enough, or else the wrong kind of justice, would have to argue in a higher court than Lincoln had ever practiced in. "As was said three thousand years ago, so still it must be said, 'The judgments of the Lord are true and righteous altogether.'"

Confronting post-slavery racism

The call for reparations for slavery is not, I believe, an ignoble one. But to the extent that it ignores the finger Lincoln points at the Civil War—to the extent that it forgets the decimation of a generation of young Americans at the beginnings of manhood; to the extent that it forgets the windrows of corpses at Shiloh, the odor of death in the Wilderness, the walking skeletons of Andersonville, 623,000 dead all told, not to mention the interminable list of those crippled, orphaned, and widowed whose pensions became the single largest bill paid by the federal government for the following half-century; to the extent that it ignores how the war cost the United States $6.6 billion, rocketed the national debt from $65 million to $2.7 billion, retarded commodity growth for the next thirty years, and devalued its currency—then the call for reparations opens itself up to a charge of willful forgetfulness so massive that resentment, anger, and bitterness, rather than justice, will (I fear) be its real legacy. The evils of slavery were real evils; so were the deaths of boy after boy, white and black, blue and gray, as well as the lag of postwar wages for Northern workers and the pauperization of Southern agriculture. In whose balances shall we say the one fails to measure up to the other?

We have also had other evils—among them, the long, disgraceful history of segregation and Jim Crow [laws that enforced segregation and denied voting rights to blacks], of lynch mob and race riot. And in that history, we confront a second case for reparations, a case that I believe needs hearing and satisfying. I believe that it is not beyond our reach or our imaginations as a nation to design a national educational trust for African-Americans which will fund the real educational opportunities that form the first rung in the ladder of American mobility, a ladder that segregation and racism made sure was the first thing stolen from African-Americans after Lincoln's death.

But this is not the same issue as slavery. For that long bill, as Lincoln rightly noted, a precious price has already been paid.

Organizations to Contact

The editors have compiled the following list of organizations concerned with the issues debated in this book. The descriptions are derived from materials provided by the organizations. All have publications or information available for interested readers. The list was compiled on the date of publication of the present volume; names, addresses, phone and fax numbers, and e-mail and Internet addresses may change. Be aware that many organizations may take several weeks or longer to respond to inquiries, so allow as much time as possible.

African American Jewish Coalition for Justice (AAJCJ)
PO Box 22843, Seattle, WA 98122-0843
e-mail: aajcj@aajcj.org • website: www.aajcj.org

The AAJCJ is a group of African and Jewish Americans who have joined in a coalition to fight racial and ethnic discrimination in the United States. The group asserts that slavery reparations will heal America's racial divide and provide African Americans with more social and economic opportunities. It publishes the monthly online newsletter *Coalition Connection* and posts member articles, such as "Reparations: An Issue of Justice and Much More," on its website.

All for Reparations and Emancipation (AFRE)
PO Box 57048, Atlanta, GA 30343
e-mail: hakimida@aol.com • website: www.afre-ngo.com

AFRE is an organization that is working to achieve a United Nations resolution condemning Western nations for their role in the slave trade. Members maintain that reparations should be paid to all peoples of African descent. AFRE's website offers links to numerous pro-reparations papers presented to the United Nations.

American Enterprise Institute (AEI)
1150 17th St. NW, Washington, DC 20036
(202) 862-5800 • fax: (202) 862-7177
e-mail: info@aei.org • website: www.aei.org

The AEI is a conservative policy and research think tank that maintains that U.S. citizens will benefit from lower taxes and less government interference in their lives. The group contends that paying slavery reparations to African Americans is wrong and will undermine personal responsibility and initiative. It publishes the magazine *American Enterprise* and numerous policy and research reports.

Caucasians United for Reparations and Emancipation (CURE)
e-mail: hakimida@aol.com • website: www.reparationsthecure.org

CURE is an organization of white Americans who contend that the U.S. government must pay reparations to the descendants of African slaves to undue the lasting harm of slavery. The group conducts educational lectures and partners with African American leaders to promote the reparations cause. Articles written by CURE members are posted on the website.

Center for the Study of Popular Culture (CSPC)
4401 Wilshire Blvd., 4th Floor, Los Angeles, CA 90010
website: www.cspc.org; www.frontpagemagazine.com

The CSPC was founded to challenge the radical leftism its members argue is endemic in American universities and media outlets. Its president, David Horowitz, is a leading critic of the slavery reparations movement. The CSPC distributes the book *Uncivil War: The Controversy over Reparations for Slavery* and numerous anti-reparations articles through its online journal, frontpagemagazine.com.

Hoover Institution
Stanford University, Stanford, CA 94305-6010
(650) 723-1754 • fax: (650) 723-1687
e-mail: horaney@hoover.stanford.edu • website: www.hoover.stanford.edu

The Hoover Institution is a conservative think tank affiliated with Stanford University. It promotes the ideals of economic and political freedom and free enterprise. The institute takes the position that slavery was perpetrated by Africans as well as by whites and therefore no restitution is due to African Americans. It publishes the quarterly *Hoover Digest* and articles and essays arguing against the reparations campaign.

National Black United Front (NBUF)
40 Clinton St., Newark, NJ 07102
(800) 223-0866
e-mail: nbuf@nbuf.org • website: www.nbuf.org

The NBUF offers financial and technical assistance to organizations that provide health care, education, economic development, and social justice to African Americans. The group collaborates and supports African American political leaders, attorneys, and academics who are actively involved in the slavery reparations campaign.

National Coalition of Blacks for Reparations in America (N'COBRA)
PO Box 90604, Washington, DC 20090-0604
(202) 291-8400 • fax: (202) 291-4600
e-mail: NationalNCOBRA@aol.com • website: www.ncobra.com

N'COBRA is a coalition of organizations and individuals who assert that the U.S. government owes African Americans trillions of dollars in reparations for the unpaid labor of their slave ancestors. To achieve this goal, N'COBRA sponsors regional and national meetings on reparations to educate the African American community. The coalition also supports the passage of H.R. 40, the reparations study bill introduced into Congress in 1989 by Michigan congressman John Conyers Jr.

New Panther Vanguard Movement (NPVM)
1470 Martin Luther King Blvd., Los Angeles, CA 90062
(323) 296-4383 • fax: (323) 296-1645
e-mail: nvpm@globalpanther.com • website: www.globalpanther.com

The NPVM is a left-wing African American group that seeks slavery reparations from the U.S. government to redress the poverty, crime, and educational failure evident in the black community. It publishes the book *Our Case for an Intercommunal Reparations Campaign* and the quarterly newspaper the *Black Panther*, accessible from the group's website.

Reason Public Policy Institute (RPPI)
3415 S. Sepulveda Blvd., Suite 400, Los Angeles, CA 90034
(310) 391-2245 • fax: (310) 391-4395
e-mail: feedback@reason.org • website: www.rppi.org

The RPPI is a research organization that supports less government interference in the lives of Americans. Their libertarian philosophy stands firmly opposed to the idea of slavery reparations; the RPPI contends that more government handouts will drain personal initiative and unfairly increase the tax burden on citizens who bear no responsibility for slavery. The institute has published articles critical of the reparations movement in the monthly magazine *Reason.*

TransAfrica Forum
1426 21st St. NW, Washington, DC 20036
(202) 223-1960 • fax: (202) 223-1966
e-mail: info@transafricaforum.org • website: www.transafricaforum.org

TransAfrica Forum conducts research on U.S. foreign policy and its effect on African peoples in Latin America, the Caribbean, and the African continent. The Forum is a leader in the movement to win slavery reparations for Africans from the U.S. government. It posts reports and papers in support of these efforts on its website including "The Case for Black Reparations" and "Slavery: Resource List." Links to numerous articles on reparations are also available.

Bibliography

Books

Elazar Barkan
The Guilt of Nations: Restitution and Negotiating Historical Injustices. New York: W.W. Norton & Company, 2000.

Roy L. Brooks, ed.
When Sorry Isn't Enough: The Controversy over Apologies and Reparations for Human Injustice. New York: New York University Press, 1999.

Frederick Douglass
Life and Times of Frederick Douglass. Secaucus, NJ: Citadel Press, 1983.

W.E. Burghardt Du Bois
Black Reconstruction. New York: Russell & Russell, 1935.

Joe R. Feagin
Racist America: Roots, Current Realities, and Future Reparations. New York: Routledge, 2000.

David Horowitz
Uncivil Wars: The Controversy over Reparations for Slavery. San Francisco: Encounter Books, 2002.

Stetson Kennedy
After Appomattox: How the South Won the War. Gainesville: University Press of Florida, 1995.

Frank McGlynn and Seymour Drescher, eds.
The Meaning of Freedom: Economics, Politics, and Culture After Slavery. Pittsburgh, PA: University of Pittsburg Press, 1992.

John H. McWhorter
Losing the Race: Self-Sabotage in Black America. New York: Free Press, 2000.

Clarence J. Munford
Race and Reparations: A Black Perspective for the 21st Century. Lawrenceville, NJ: Africa World Press, 1996.

Claude F. Oubre
Forty Acres and a Mule: The Freedmen's Bureau and Black Land Ownership. Baton Rouge: Louisiana State University Press, 1978.

Randall Robinson
The Debt: What America Owes to Blacks. New York: Dutton, 2000.

George Schedler
Racist Symbols and Reparations: Philosophical Reflections on Vestiges of the American Civil War. Lanham, MD: Rowman & Littlefield, 1998.

T.J. Stiles, ed.
In Their Own Words: Robber Barons and Radicals. New York: Perigree, 1997.

Raymond A. Winbush, ed.
Should America Pay?: Slavery and the Raging Debate on Reparations. New York: Amistad, 2003.

Periodicals

Richard F. America   "Reparations and Higher Education," *Black Issues in Higher Education*, January 6, 2000.

Steven P. Benenson   "Suits Are Too Little, Too Late," *National Law Journal*, May 13, 2002.

Anthony Gifford   "The Legal Basis of the Claim for Slavery Reparations," *Human Rights*, Spring 2000.

Hakim Hasan   "Reparation Anxiety," *City Limits*, August 31, 2002.

Rodney G. Hood   "The 'Slave Health Deficit': The Case for Reparations to Bring Health Parity to African Americans," *Journal of the National Medical Association*, January 2001.

Horace Huntley   "Generations of Unpaid Labor Make a Case for Reparations," *Black Collegian*, February 2002.

Earl Ofari Hutchinson   "Ten Reasons Why Considering Reparations Is a Good Idea for Americans and Horowitz Too," *Poverty & Race*, June 30, 2001.

Manning Marable   "Reparations and Our Rendezvous with History," *Peacework Magazine*, February 28, 2002.

Bob McLalan   "How I Changed My Mind," *Sojourners*, March/April 2001.

Deroy Murdock   "A Bean Counting Nightmare to Avoid," *American Enterprise*, July/August 2001.

Charles Ogletree Jr.   "Reparations, a Fundamental Issue of Social Justice," *Black Collegian*, October 2002.

Charles Ogletree Jr. and E.R. Shipp   "Does America Owe Us? Point/Counterpoint," *Essence*, February 2003.

Walter Olson   "Stale Claims," *Reason*, November 2000.

Adolf Reed Jr.   "The Case Against Reparations," *Progressive*, December 2000.

Ronald Roach   "Fighting the Good Fight," *Black Issues in Higher Education*, November 8, 2001.

Randall Robinson   "America's Debt to Blacks," *Nation*, March 13, 2000.

Randall Robinson and Armstrong Williams   "Symposium: Payment of Reparations to the Descendants of Slaves," *Insight on the News*, January 1, 2001.

Thomas Sowell   "The Modern Tragedy of 'Roots,'" *Human Events*, February 4, 2002.

Shelby Steele   ". . . Or Childish Illusion of Justice? Reparations Enshrine Victimhood, Dishonoring Our Ancestors," *Newsweek*, August 27, 2001.

Ronald Walters   "For Slavery?: Let's Resolve the Inequity," *World and I*, April 2000.

Woody West	"The Absurdity of Black Reparations," *Insight on the News*, February 5, 2001.
Jack E. White	"Don't Waste Your Breath," *Time*, April 2, 2001.
Walter E. Williams	"Reparations for 'Legacy of Slavery' Just Another Hustle," *Human Events*, June 18, 2001.
Walter E. Williams	"Reparations for Slavery an Immoral Idea," *Human Events*, July 28, 2000.

Internet Sources

Black Reparations.com
website: www.blackreparations.com

All sides in the reparations debate are presented on this website, which includes access to articles, research, surveys, and discussion groups.

National Review Online
website: www.nationalreview.com

This conservative online magazine has published articles critical of the slavery reparations campaign including "The U.N.'s Racism Sham," August 1, 2001, by Rich Lowry.

Reparations Central
e-mail: greg@carey.net • website: www.reparationscentral.com

Reparations Central is an online clearinghouse of proreparations articles, video clips, and legal updates. The site provides links to numerous organizations involved in the reparations campaign.

Index